POOPY FINGERS

One Person's Account of Working in the Delightfully Strange World of Assisted Living

D1572204

BY
KEVIN DONNER

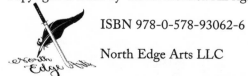

CONTENTS

CHAPTER ZERO

Rediscovering the Most
Wonderfully Heartbreaking
Year of My Life

Think back to your childhood. Try to remember your favorite possessions at various ages. Whether we were rich or poor, or anywhere along that spectrum in between, most of us had something that we loved. Perhaps when you were six, it was a picture book that you couldn't put down; when you were eight, it was a particular stuffed animal that you loved until it was all matted, with its stuffing falling out; and when you were ten, it was a Lego set that you received as a birthday present, and when finished putting it together, you put it up on your shelf like a prized athletic trophy.

For me, some of those items that stand out to this day are a small stuffed monkey whose hands and feet were filled with sand so that it could hang off of things, a kaleidoscope, and a Raffi record that I received as a birthday present one year and listened to incessantly.

Now, try to remember what happened to these items. Sure, you may recall a specific incident where something was broken, or just maybe you still have some of them. I still have that kaleidoscope! However, in most cases, and in all likelihood, these items just seem to have vanished from our childhoods. Perhaps, for many of you, if I hadn't asked you to delve back, you may have gone the rest of your lives never thinking back to that favorite sweater or board game.

What happened to them?

Where did they go?

It wasn't until years later, when I became a parent, that I learned the true fate of all those seemingly irreplaceable belongings. When you were away at school, at a friend's house for a playdate, or otherwise not paying attention, your parents or guardians boxed them up and either gave them away to someone else's children, donated them to charity, or simply threw them in the trash.

That boxing up of toys, and other random items, is where this story continues. I say continues and not begins because this manuscript was written fourteen years ago, and then subsequently forgotten about. We've moved quite a bit, including twice across country, and many of our possessions have stayed in the moving boxes in which they were long ago placed. I recently rediscovered this manuscript in a box of dusty broken toys, ethernet cables, and various obsolete technology that I had forgotten I had even ever owned. Perhaps some of those toys are ones whose fate my son may someday wonder about.

How could I have forgotten about something I spent so much time and energy writing? I never intended to seek publication for the following story. The act of committing it to paper was more akin to a debriefing following an intense, life-altering ordeal. I had never been a journal keeper, but I felt crippled by the overwhelming need to record the following experiences while they were still actively affecting me from within. I needed to take stock of myself, the life I had lived up until that point, and the tone I wanted to set for the years I still had ahead of me. This manuscript chronicles the year I spent working in the wonderful, painful, exciting, joyous, and strange world of assisted living. Working in assisted living had been a beautiful accident for me, but that is only part of this story.

This manuscript was heartbreaking for me to reread after so much time had passed. While it sat undisturbed at the bottom of a moving box, most of the people who occupy its pages, already in their eighties or nineties at the time of its writing, have now long since passed away.

In the years that have passed between then and now, the world did what it does best. It kept spinning, taking us all along for the ride. This manuscript was long since forgotten by the time I had discovered Facebook, bought my first smartphone, or knew what Wi-Fi was. My son, with whom my wife was pregnant when I wrote this, is now fourteen, and we now also have two daughters. Along with that, my hair is going gray.

I am also reminded of how lucky I was to work in senior care when I did. We're now in the midst of a global pandemic that is leaving no person on this planet unaffected in some profound way. As is evident, the elderly are more likely to die from COVID-19 than other members of our society, and so many people seem willing to sacrifice the elderly so that life can more quickly return to normal for the rest of us. The senior care industry may never be the same again. In facilities like Gleeful Meadows, where I worked in the following pages, all activities and visitations have been cancelled for more than a year due to the danger of spreading COVID-19, and there is no way of knowing when, or if, life within nursing homes, assisted living, and other long-term care facilities will ever return to something resembling normalcy. I remember so vividly offering up hugs to our senior residents, though this simple gesture now seems like something from the barely remembered distant past.

Rereading these pages, I was reminded of many happy memories. There were many sad ones too. Rereading my experiences also reminded me of Former Vice President Hubert Humphrey's quote: "The moral test of government is how that government treats those who are in the dawn of life, the children; those who are in the twilight of life, the elderly; those who are in the shadows of life, the sick, the needy and the handicapped."

So how do the following pages relate to you, and why am I sharing them? I think the most succinct answer to both these questions is simply that each and every one of us, regardless of color or creed, is one day going to die. Some sooner than others, some easier than others. If we are lucky enough to live a long, happy, and healthy life, these pages contain a small glimpse into what one might expect during those later years. It's not all roses, nor is it all thorns. Just like all the years that preceded, life is a bag of mixed nuts.

Let's all take care of one another.

--Kevin Donner 7/24/21

CHAPTER ONE

Oh, to Be Young Again

The bag of pee strapped to his ankle was what most people noticed first about Ariel S. For a man shrinking at an alarming rate—he had most recently measured in at 4 foot 11—his clothing, for some inexplicable reason, was shrinking faster than he was. The result being that, instead of shrinking, Ariel thought that he was in fact growing. Each morning when the care staff dressed him, he marveled at his latest apparent growth spurt. Each pair of pants barely reached down to his ankles. His belt buckle, pants button, and zipper were always disengaged. The only thing that kept people from seeing the other end of the urine bag, which was attached to his penis by a catheter, was the pair of faded red suspenders that had been with Ariel nearly every day of his adult life.

"Am I going through some sort of a growth spurt?" he would ask. "Is this normal? Is something wrong with me? How tall will I get?"

The care staff, on the other hand, wondered how small he and his clothing would become. Whether one day he would need to go naked— as he both refused to buy new clothes nor to wear anything that he had not brought with him to Gleeful Meadows Assisted Living—or whether they would come to his room to wake him one morning and he would not be there, having grown too small for his neutrons and protons to hold him together at all.

Ariel was not without his charm. The only problem was that most people had a very difficult time discovering it, as it required actually spending time with him. People were usually repelled or repulsed long before that time of discovery arrived. Ariel was on "behavior watch," as dictated by the nursing director. The most recent of his indiscretions, which were always verbal and never physical, was to tell his caregiver during his shower session that she needed to clean his penis twice. The first cleaning being for the normal wear and tear of daily living, and the second cleaning was for what he had fantasized using it for.

On the sidewalk in front of a donut shop, Ariel laid his arms over the front of his walker. He looked again for a place to sit. The curbs were all too low for him to lower himself onto. He had tried to rest upon the bumper of a parked car, which had then started to make a piercing high-pitched noise.

He could see clearly perhaps five feet in front of himself. Beyond that, the parking lot turned into a blur, mixed with the sky and horizon into a blended abstract. His glasses hung around his neck via a piece of string, so naturally he assumed that he had forgotten them at home. Wherever home might be. He could never remember. He wasn't crazy, or at least he didn't think he was. After all, he knew his own name and his social security number—well, most of it, anyway.

As with most of the residents who called Gleeful Meadows their home, I had learned some of Ariel's earlier life and experiences over hot chocolate or coffee. Ariel had worked every day of his life from his fifteenth birthday until his eighty-eighth. On that day, he had said that he was tired. He stopped getting out of bed for meals, stopped grooming himself, and stopped taking pleasure in those things which used to give him pleasure. In truth, nobody knew what those things were, but it was evident that, whatever they had been, they were no longer doing their job. So, Ariel's son did what most people would do in his situation—found a place where his father would be cared for and would not be allowed to starve or wallow in his own filth.

"Yeah, it's really nice that he gets to live out his golden years in this cushy place with me footing the bill," Ariel's son had said to me. "He didn't pay for a goddamn thing while I was growing up. He was a lousy father. He never hit us, but he never hugged us either. Barely saw him. The man was never there."

I hear that he was too busy earning a living putting food on the table, I thought to myself.

I pulled the bus to a stop in front of Safeway, once again employing a liberal use of unlawful parking spaces, which I felt were made slightly less unlawful by the handicap decal that rested on my dashboard.

I entered the coffee shop at the front of the store and saw my group waiting for me with their assorted purchases. A potted plant in the lap of one wheelchair-bound resident caught my eye. Potting soil already covered the front of her blouse, culminating in small mounds around the base of the pot on her skirt, as well as a dark trail ground into the floor that marked her path. I also looked with disdain at the full grocery cart next to another resident, knowing that I was the one who would have to carry her purchases into the bus, secure them, then later carry them off to her room, storing them in her cupboards and icebox. Gleeful Meadows Assisted Living, where I worked as the activities director, provided three meals a day, as well as snacks. Why anyone wouldn't take advantage of that—considering that they were already paying for it—was beyond me. I was even taking advantage of it and had already gained ten pounds since I began working there.

I took a headcount. "Adeline, where's Iris?" I asked.

"How would I know?"

"You said you'd keep her with you."

"She wanted to look at the candy bars."

"I told you she needed to be watched. You said okay."

"After she veered down aisle six, she was out of my hands. Does it look like I need another candy bar?" She flashed a grin that revealed her three remaining teeth, one of which was so decayed and porous that it took on the color of her most recent meal. At the moment, it was a light shade of blue. Adeline S was a heavy-set woman who never wore anything other than a cream-colored knit sweater and matching pair of sweatpants that were so tightly wrapped around her meaty thighs that I wondered if, years earlier, she had just given up trying to take them off. Her gray hair was in ringlets and sported two plastic barrettes, the kind a little girl would wear.

"Everyone wait here," I said. I ran to the candy aisle and saw Iris H midway down the aisle with her hands filled with chocolate bars. I rushed to her.

"Iris, you had me worried."

"How could I worry you?" She tugged on her yellow mullet and adjusted her enormous glasses.

"Our friends are waiting for us at the front."

"Which friends?"

"You'll see."

"I've got to go to the little girl's room," she said.

"Supermarket restrooms are dirty. Can you wait until we get home?"

"I suppose. Who's going to pay for all this?" I looked at all the candy she had.

"We've got candy at home." That was a half truth. The full truth was that we did, in fact, have plenty of candy back at the community, but Iris was not allowed to have any. Her daughter was convinced that she was getting a little too round and, therefore, wanted us to restrict her sweets intake. I did my best to look in the other direction when such intake was taking place. My personal point of view was that, if a woman going on ninety wanted to end her days in a chocolate bliss overdose, well then, who am I to stand in the way of such a delightful exit?

However, buying her what she now held would be a blatant disregard of her family's wishes, and besides, we were running short on time. I was new at the job, but I had already discovered that the world of assisted living revolved around the punctual start and stop of daily activities. Our "trip to Safeway" was nearing its finishing point, and "cooking with Kevin" (that's me) needed to begin promptly in twenty minutes. If it didn't, no doubt a phone call would be made to the ombudsman by one of the eighty-six residents describing the "flagrant disregard for scheduled activities—not to mention the walls which haven't been painted in over two years, and the soup was served lukewarm two weeks ago, and would it kill Gleeful Meadows to serve prawns instead of shrimp, and I think that they didn't pass out the mail until after dinner time last Monday, which is clearly a violation of our civil rights, and I also noticed a trace of mildew in my shower which could be a biohazard issue that the state authorities might have to look into."

I did not want to be the cause, or even appear to be the cause, of one of those phone calls *again*.

"Has anyone seen Ariel?" I asked once back at the coffee shop area with Iris.

"Who?"

"Red hat with his name on it. Sits next to you at dinner."

"Never heard of him."

"I don't like him. He's rude," someone else said.

"It's definitely rude of him to be late."

I led the group outside. "I'm going to have you all wait on the bus while I look for him." I checked my watch and opened the doors to the bus. The able-bodied residents began filing on as I went around to the back to operate the wheelchair lift. After I had loaded and secured my one current passenger with a wheelchair, I walked back around the front of the bus to see Adeline struggling to pull herself up the stair rail.

"I've got the lift ready for you," I said.

"I want to try the stairs."

"Are you sure? Didn't you take a tumble a couple of weeks ago?"

"That was different. I was rushing then because I really had to use the toilet."

"You're sure you want to do this?"

"Absolutely."

In our line of work, we try to encourage as much independence as possible. The physical and psychological benefits are obvious. The pitfalls are obvious only to those of us who have walked these paths on repeated occasions. Even though I was relatively new at my post, certain experiences had made me a hardened veteran, and I knew from those experiences that I was heading face-first into one of the job's pitfalls.

As Adeline gripped the base of the railing leading up into the bus, I positioned myself behind her with my arms ready to support her weight in the event that her legs could not. She began to pull herself upward. The sound of aged exertion was the warning I was waiting for. I turned my head away from the pitfall—preferring to encounter it ear first.

Three...two...one...

The sound of the fart was wet, though luckily most of the sound, and much of its aromatic value, were absorbed by Adeline's adult diaper. She moved forward into the bus, and I followed, holding my breath.

There are side effects of aging that one can't describe without seeming to be making light of them. Laughing at the humors of aging is not the same as making jokes about them. Prior to coming to work with seniors, I would have turned my nose up at such a description if I had read it. Looking back, I learned more life lessons than I can remember in my year of working amongst the aged, and one of them was taught to me by a resident who had sneezed and inadvertently peed herself. "If we don't laugh, we cry. So, we might as well do both at once." I try to remember that always.

"Are we going to miss bingo?" someone asked.

"Bingo's tomorrow," someone else replied.

"Can't we play it today?"

"Then what will we do tomorrow?"

Once everyone was locked securely inside the bus, I ran back inside Safeway and searched the aisles, though I did not find Ariel.

I stood on the curb with my hands on my hips. A bus full of seniors looked down at me, some probably wondering how they could help, others wondering if we would be home in time for dinner, and still others wondering why I looked so familiar.

I boarded the bus and then drove the length of the strip mall, glancing at the pedestrians, hoping that one of them would match the description of my quarry. None did. When I reached the far end of the final shop, I turned left so that I could make a loop of the parking lot, allowing me to come back around for another pass. Taking the long route would be quicker and less taxing than making a three-point turn. In this bus, a three-point turn more readily offered the driver the prospect of finding himself wedged impossibly between opposite curbs, as well as marring the already scuffed paint job with love-taps from a variety of objects that all lay concealed by the design of the bus, which had more blind spots than sides.

To my knowledge, I had never met anyone suffering from Alzheimer's disease before coming to work at Gleeful Meadows. About fifty percent of our residents had a diagnosis of Alzheimer's, and an additional thirty percent suffered from some form of dementia resulting from other illnesses. This is a population that can take some getting used to. Some people never get used to it. Industry statistics say that the average yearly turnover rate for staff in assisted living is *a hundred and thirty-three* percent. Of course, there are many wonderful people who find their passion in a lifelong career in this beautiful industry, but there are many, many more who try it and then run screaming. In one year, I saw two executive directors, three business managers, four receptionists, four care staff managers, three marketing directors, and four activity directors pass through Gleeful Meadows. This list doesn't include the plethora of support staff working under those directors who I saw come and go, and go and go.

Bottom line, it's an industry that quickly weeds out those who don't truly have a passion for it. Working with Alzheimer's can be scary and sad. It can also be incredibly fun and funny. Once again, there is nothing wrong with allowing ourselves to see the humor in sickness. Anyone who works in a stressful industry will tell you that the only way to cope is to laugh. Ask a family member of an individual suffering from Alzheimer's, and, more often than not, they will tell you that it's not just okay to laugh—it's necessary.

As I drove, I considered employing the assistance of the minds and eyes that sat behind me. Even though the majority of them suffered from at least mild dementia, they tended to be more aware of their surroundings than one might readily believe or even hope. However, with that said, the collected effect of their voices and experiences tended more readily to follow the mob rule phenomenon of breaking down the collective to its lowest common denominator rather than being elevated by a meeting of the minds and a "more heads are better than one" outcome.

"Where are we going?"

"We're lost."

"We're not lost, somebody else is."

"I think we're all here."

"Are we going shopping?"

"Did you take a head count?"

"We're not going shopping, we just came from there."

"Who's paying for this?"

"Kevin, are you going to get fired?"

"My kids never got lost, because I never let them out on their own."

"Whose kid is lost?"

"Somebody lost their kid?"

"What kind of a parent would lose their kid?"

"My kids never got lost, because I never let them out on their own."

"Aren't we going the wrong way? The shopping center is back there."

"I think we lost somebody."

"Are we going out for lunch? I didn't bring my wallet."

"My kids just dumped me off here and left me. They made it seem like we was going on a little get-away. They said, 'Isn't this a nice place?' Then I noticed it was all my things in the room. I said, 'What's going on here?' They said, 'This is your new home.'"

"My kids never got lost, because I never let them out on their own."

And on and on it went as I drove.

I checked my watch. How long could I search before I needed to call my boss to tell him that "one of the eggs has fallen from the basket?" A call certainly worse than "one of the eggs has cracked and is now leaking all over the bus" (quite common, indeed), but not as bad as "Sir, one of the eggs is dead."

It was now time to take the search to the street—store by store by store. I was scared and beginning to panic and not thinking straight.

I thumbed my cell phone in my pocket, delaying my shame coming to light.

I entered Target, and for the first time in my life, was overwhelmed by its immensity. Where once I reveled in the "hell yeah" attitude of having every possible shape, size, color, and brand of every product I could imagine available to me under one roof, I now cursed at the nooks, crannies, aisles, doorways, hallways, innies and outies, and stock galore that possibly stood between me and Ariel. Assuming that he was even in here and not at Buster's Cameras, Toro's Teriyaki, or a thousand other stores in between.

There are several things that one must keep in mind when hunting down a missing senior, a list I made up while I walked to the customer service counter.

1. Remove your name tag.
2. Lock the others in the bus. I'm not exactly sure of the legal implications of this step, but I feared the possibility of losing

another resident much more than I did that of a spontaneous bus explosion.

3.   Never have a store employee announce the individual's name over the loudspeaker. The reason for this is two-fold.

     a.   You want to keep this as clandestine as possible.

     b.   A lost senior is not like a lost child. They will not bound up to the customer service station upon hearing their name. There's a good chance that their hearing aids are not even on and, therefore, they will not hear the aforementioned announcement, which could leave you standing there for a very long, fruitless, and wasted amount of time. Furthermore, seniors *do not* bound.

No matter how nervous you might be, never show it. Pretend like everything is cool. Store clerks can smell fear.

"I'm looking for an elderly man in a red ball cap," I said.

The staffer, a girl of perhaps sixteen, glanced down at my chest, and I realized I had neglected to employ the first step on my list. "What's Gleeful Meadows?" she asked. "Sounds like a funeral home."

I wondered for a moment if I had neglected to also lock the doors of the bus, and an image of aimlessly wandering seniors being clipped down by cars in the parking lot, entertained itself upon my psyche for the briefest of moments. The girl turned to an older, plumper version of herself at the far end of the counter, who was scanning returned items with a tool that looked like a magic wand. "This guy's lost his grandfather." She turned back to me and shrugged. "A lot of people pass this counter. It's a busy place."

"It would have taken him considerable time to pass this counter. I mean, he moves really, really slow. You would have had plenty of opportunity to notice him."

She took hold of a microphone. "What's his name?" she asked me.

"He won't hear you if you call him with that."

"So, what do you want me to do?"

I left the counter shaking my head. Crap. I'd have to run through the entire store. Ten minutes later I was sweaty and still hadn't found Ariel. I began to worry that he had gotten hurt. Lost was one thing. Lost can be fixed with found. But hurt, on the other hand. If he had fallen…or…. A worse thought came to mind. Not death, but what if someone had decided he looked like an easy mark for a scam? Losing his life savings to someone's unscrupulousness could have happened many times over by now in the time since I had last seen him.

I had seen this sort of thing before. The first time was even before I began working with seniors. I had been in line at a bank and had overheard as the teller described to a woman and her elderly mother how the old woman's bank account had been drained by a young companion of hers whom she had trusted, whom she had thought was her only friend in the world. For some time, the old woman couldn't seem to grasp what had happened, but when understanding, and then shame, came to her, she said that she wished she could just die.

Could that sort of thing be happening to Ariel right now? I admitted to myself that it was unlikely, as most of our residents had long since relinquished control of their finances to their children. But this wasn't always the case, and even when it was, the circumstances were often less than ideal. We'll come back to that later.

Back on the bus, I took a moment to gather my thoughts. My store-to-store search had turned up nothing. I was no longer just afraid for myself and getting in trouble. I was now deeply afraid for Ariel and the trouble that he was no doubt already in.

"I'm out of options," I said.

"You act as though you've never lost anyone before," someone said.

"Just glad it wasn't me," someone else said.

"Who's lost?"

I drove slowly back toward the entrance of Safeway. Beyond that was the entrance to the parking lot, a line I did not want to cross, perhaps ever again. I withdrew my cell phone and pressed the speed dial for Gleeful Meadows.

A car behind us began to honk its horn. I looked in my side mirror and saw the car (I never was very good at specific vehicular identification) swerving left and right. "What's his problem?" I asked. The phone rang.

"What a jackass," someone said behind me in the bus. Assuming he wanted to get past me, I rolled down my window and waved him through. He did not pass, but merely kept honking and swerving side to side.

"Did you run someone over?" one of my seniors asked.

The call was picked up on the second ring. "Good afternoon, Gleeful Meadows," a charming female voice said.

"Hey, it's me. I need to talk to Paul."

"What's wrong?"

"I lost Ariel."

"Oh no. Hold on, I'll put you through to him. Good luck." I was put on hold.

The car behind us continued to swerve and honk. "That young man's parents should have taught him to be more respectful of people," someone said.

"My kids never got lost, because I never let them out on their own."

Shut up, shut up, shut up, I thought.

I again waved the person to pass, but the honking continued.

The on-hold music coming in over my cell phone stopped. "This is Paul."

"Ariel's in the car," someone shouted. "Stop the bus, Ariel's in the car."

I held the phone away from my face. "What was that?" I yelled back.

"He stole a car?" someone else asked.

"No, he's in the passenger seat."

"Hello?" I heard Paul's voice say. I pressed the end call button and put the phone back in my pocket.

I pulled the bus to a stop and got out. The driver of the car did the same. I could see Ariel sitting in the front passenger seat, now fumbling with the door.

"Thank God," I said. "Where did you find him?"

"Wandering in the parking lot," the man said. He walked around the car and opened the door. I rushed to his side to help Ariel to his feet. The Samaritan removed Ariel's walker from the back seat. As soon as Ariel was free from the car, he threw his arms around me and pressed his face into my chest. At first, I thought he had lost his balance, but then I realized that this was an action he had intended. As deliberate as it was reflexive. Ariel needed to be comforted, needed to be held and reassured that everything was alright. His body shook violently with sobs of both fear and relief.

As Ariel cried in my arms, the smell of his aftershave reminded me of something. Two days prior, I had had a disagreement with our head nurse regarding Ariel's appearance when he leaves the facility on outings such as this one. Typically, his ensemble included a white dress shirt, blazer, and bathrobe all covered in various articles of mouth-missed food. Once I had seen the thick, gooey innards of a blueberry pie resting precariously on the inside edge of his open shirt. I had mentioned this to him, and before I could reach forward and rescue the blueberry mash, Ariel patted his shirt down, smooshing the bluey-gooey goodness into his shirt, and causing most of it to fall back down in between his inner and outer shirts.

The nurse had argued that, with concern for the marketable image of the facility, we should require Ariel be clothed cleanly and smartly before leaving the property on outings. I had felt in my gut that this was not fair, though I had a difficult time, as is often the case, articulating my feelings in a coherent, non-stammering fashion. I knew I was right, though I didn't know exactly how or why.

Presently, as I stood on the sidewalk with Ariel in my arms, and the Samaritan next to us, the thesis of my argument at once became clear to me. We should be vigilant about the appearance of our residents when they leave the property, not because their appearance is a reflection upon us, but because their appearance is a reflection upon themselves. It was not the endgame of the nurse's argument that I had found so objectionable, but merely the reason behind it. Ariel's dignity was of chief importance, not our marketability. He should be shaved, showered, combed, in clean and fresh clothing, because that is what's best for *him*, and if that's what also happens to be best for our facility, well, then, that was just a bonus. I knew that the reality of the world also dictated that, if Ariel had been lost in the parking lot, looking as disheveled as he usually did, he would most likely still be there, and I would be on the phone right now explaining to Paul that I had lost one of my precious cargo. Appearance is everything.

Back at Gleeful Meadows, as the residents filed from the bus, Dorothea M gave me a hug. "Thank you so much for taking us to the store, Kevin."

Cora D, off the bus right behind her, complained, "Hey, how come I didn't get to go to the store? No one told me you were going."

"I'm so sorry, Cora. I don't know what I was thinking. I'll make a special point of making sure you're on the bus the next time we go." That moment, right there, was my job. Making them happy. Sometimes it required fixing them a cup of tea. Sometimes it required taking them to the store. Other times it required filling in the gaps of their memories that their illnesses had left behind. Lies filled the holes just as easily as the memories that had slipped away from them. I was here to help create new memories, no matter how fleeting they might be.

That evening, before I left work for the day, I paid a visit to Ariel's room. After a moment's hesitation, I knocked on the door. I waited a beat, and then entered the room. Ariel was sitting on his bed in his robe, his head in his hands. The room was lit by a small nightlight plugged into a wall socket. He looked up at me and smiled. "Hey, it's the Jewish kid," he said.

"I was thinking the same about you."

"What can I help you with?" he asked.

"Can I come in?"

"Does it look like I've got much else going on?"

"No date tonight?"

"I thought I'd give the ladies a break."

"I'm sure they appreciate it." I sat next to him on the bed. "Are you okay?" I asked.

"I'm in perfect health. As long as you don't count the eight or ten things wrong with me."

"No, I mean about today."

Ariel looked at me for a long moment before he spoke. During the silence, his eyes reddened and filled with tears. "Getting old isn't all bad. Though it's true you spend a lot of time thinking about the past. Wishing you could do some things over again. Or wishing you could undo some things completely.

"Today was the first time that I had ever noticed my memory isn't what it used to be. When I was in that parking lot, I couldn't remember the name of this goddamn place, or the phone number, let alone what store we were supposed to meet at. Christ, I've spent so much time wishing I were young again. Today, I finally got my wish, and it wasn't what I had hoped for."

"What do you mean?"

"You ever get lost as a kid?"

"Sure."

"That's what I was today. A lost kid. That feeling all over again. Right back like it was yesterday. The world too damn big and me too damn small to understand a thing." He lowered his head back into his hands.

It's been said that we never stop learning, as long as we're above ground. That day, I learned that everything I cherish in my life, I take for granted: health, family, independence, and a feeling of self-worth. I saw how quickly, or even slowly and surreptitiously, those things can be stripped from a person.

Another thing I would learn that day was that my wife was pregnant. I was going to be a father.

"I suppose, after today, you're not in a huge rush to get back out to the store with me," I said to Ariel.

"Are you kidding? I'm ready to go again right now," he said.

"So soon?"

Ariel smiled. "At my age, you can't plan any further ahead than that."

CHAPTER TWO

Some Then and Now

Some years earlier, when my wife, Angie, graduated from medical school, we moved to a town two hours north of Sydney, Australia, called Newcastle. I was excited about the move; however, this was the start of a very difficult period for the old Kevster. Newcastle, at the time, had a high rate of unemployment (relatively speaking), and I remember vividly going around to businesses in the 100-degree heat with 95% humidity to hand out resumes, most of which, by that point, were covered in sweaty palm prints. Around this time, Angie and I discussed the possibility that I alone may have to move back to Canada if employment was not forthcoming in the near future. As depression led to despair, I allowed myself a faint sliver of optimism as I was asked to attend a group interview for Australia's largest supermarket chain. For those of you unfamiliar with a group interview, imagine *American Idol* without the singing. I had to show up to the interview two hours early so that my sweat stains could dry.

I still maintain to this day that I stood out because of my Canadian accent, which, in rural Australia, was exotic. Out of forty people who walked into that office, I was the one who walked out with the job. That job, far short of glamour, was as a part-time cashier in a supermarket. A "checkout chick," as I was repeatedly referred to. The most important thing, however, was that it helped pay the bills and put some dignity back in my soul.

I learned a great deal about humility at that time in my life. A man whom I met at the interview had been out of work for nearly a year. He was in his early fifties, a factory worker, who had been laid off. I still wonder about him and how long it took him to eventually find work— or if he ever did. I think about his family too, even though I never met them. Any sense of embarrassment over working a cash register with two university degrees to my credit, while my wife saved lives, was washed away by the knowledge of what employment symbolized. Beyond a paycheck, it is a real and concrete way to show society and ourselves that we have value.

After just over a year in Newcastle, it came time for us to move once again. Angie's career had taken us from Canada to Australia, then around Australia—but family tragedies made us yearn for a home closer to our families in Vancouver, British Columbia—and that home ended up being Seattle, Washington, just a hop, skip, and a jump away. We sold most of our possessions, said our goodbyes, and boarded a plane to the United States with the same two suitcases we had arrived with in Australia years earlier.

As it was Angie's job that precipitated the move, I was the one left, once again, with the arduous task of finding work. The job I found would change my life forever.

Finding one's place usually doesn't come easily, and rarely does it come quickly. John Lennon said it best that "Life is what happens to you while you're busy making other plans." I have had a lot of different jobs. I worked in a bookstore, dressed as a giant turtle, installed emergency lighting inside a dam, worked a jackhammer, sold souvenirs, worked in a plumbing warehouse, and assembled furniture—to name just a few of the other hats I have worn on my journey.

Senior care, or more specifically assisted living, was an industry I never would have imagined could offer me any measure of satisfaction or enjoyment. In fact, I used to constantly say to Angie, whose goal since medical school was to become a geriatrician, "Who the heck would want to work with old people?"

As it turned out, I would.

I responded to an ad for a concierge at a place called Gleeful Meadows. The name sounded so positive, like everyone would be prancing through daisy-covered fields while singing songs and giggling. I wonder if that was the image they were hoping to conjure.

Gleeful Meadows was in a suburb of Seattle called Renton. I didn't know where Renton was. I didn't even know what assisted living was, or, for that matter, what a concierge was responsible for, other than getting people sweet tickets to concerts and ballgames. As fate would dictate, I was offered the job. What's funny is that, if I had known in the interview that "concierge" was merely the Gleeful Meadows euphemism for receptionist, I probably would not have accepted the position.

Thank God for false advertising!

Every day of the year I worked at Gleeful Meadows I woke up thinking firstly about how lucky I was to have a job. I would think about people like the man I met at the interview years earlier in Newcastle, Australia, who was unemployed. Then I would think about how lucky I was to work in an industry where I got to be a part of making people's lives better.

I soon learned that "assisted living" was a generic term for the vast space between fully independent active senior on the one hand and palliative bedridden vegetative invalid on the other. It was an exciting place to be, as we were the home for a spectrum that blurred slightly into both extremes—a demographic, it turned out, I really enjoyed working with.

Every morning I looked forward to getting to work, and every evening I felt a little empty leaving.

Happiness and complete fulfillment with what I was doing had found me entirely by accident. I loved the residents whom I spent my days with. They are probably the closest friends I have ever had.

Home from work, I lay on the sofa listening to my latest mix CD. In an attempt to more familiarize myself with the new and fabulous world of senior care, I looked at the advertising material for Gleeful Meadows. What a load of crap!

The brochure was filled with geriatric beauties. Who the heck were these people? Where did they live? Certainly not at Gleeful Meadows. There was nothing at all wrong with these airbrushed, silver supermodels. Their hair was always perfect white or silver, never blotchy, never missing. Their teeth, similarly, were always white, never blotchy, never missing. They all looked distinguished and regal. They never forgot where their rooms were, or who their families were. And they certainly never fell asleep in a diaper full of their own poop. Who were they to represent our residents?

I got up and went to my computer, opening the file where I had loaded the several hundred photos I had taken in the past few weeks at work. I opened PowerPoint and began importing photos of residents— missing teeth, blotchy hair, and all. Yikes, one or two may need a little airbrushing. Just a little.

"Hey," Angie's voice came from behind me.

"Hey," I said without turning around. "I didn't hear you come in."

She walked over to me and put her arms around my neck. "What are you doing?"

"Not sure yet. Sort of a slide show."

In the kitchen, we poked around in the fridge and cupboards for a midnight snack. I dipped a spoon into a jar of peanut butter.

"So, my pregnant wife, how are you feeling?"

Angie chewed on a kalamata olive. "Fine. No sickness at all."

"I still can't believe you took the test last night without me being there."

"I couldn't wait for you to get home."

"How was I supposed to know you'd ever get off early?"

"You snooze you lose, dude," she said.

"How was your day today?" I asked.

"Not bad." She leaned over and put an olive in my mouth as she said, "I did have my finger up three people's butts today!"

I dry heaved and turned to the sink to spit out the olive.

Angie laughed.

"What the hell is the matter with you?" I said.

She sniffed her fingers. "Sometimes the smell makes it through the latex. I double glove if it looks like their bum is going to be extra fragrant."

"Why are you telling me this while we're eating?"

"To toughen you up. We've got a lot of messy baby stuff ahead. I want to make sure you're ready."

"I'm toughened. I'm ready. I've listened for years to stories you've brought home of vein stripping, nasty skanky cheesy toenails, and broken light bulbs up the butt. Believe me, I'm toughened. Now I've got to wonder if I might have smelled the fecal remnants of a patient on your finger, forever ruining the pleasure of kalamata olives."

"Give me a break." Angie smelled her fingers again and laughed.

I walked down Broadway toward Domino's to pick up our pizza. I moved slowly, taking my time as I passed the sidewalk seating of restaurants. One of my favorite pastimes was to eavesdrop on conversations.

This night, however, I seemed to be even more aware of the environment around me. I felt more receptive to what the street offered. Sounds and smells and sights came at me with heightened intensity.

"Daddy, why's that man sleeping on the sidewalk?"

I turned to look at my imaginary child next to me. At this point, just an indefinable silhouette, neither boy nor girl. Was this why I seemed to be noticing things I hadn't before? Because I was going to be a father?

What would I answer to the question of people sleeping on the streets? Was there a right answer? Certainly, there had to be less-wrong answers. "He's not as lucky as us. He made bad decisions in life. He's lazy. He's crazy. He got a crap deal at some point along the way. Go ask your mother." I didn't know what to say.

Suddenly the world seemed so much more incomprehensible. I couldn't understand it myself. This realization now struck me as more of a deficiency than a natural result of being an innocent bystander in the heaving and groaning of the universe. The indefinable silhouette took further shape and became a small boy. What would I tell my son when he asked questions I didn't know the answers to?

I continued down the sidewalk at a leisurely stroll. I'd never strolled before. I'd always been a fast walker. My walk had purpose, designed to deter the most persistent and annoying downtown street corner canvasser, stating loudly, and in no uncertain terms, that I don't have time, or even a care about their cause, questions, polls, politics, or product samples. But, now, my gait was different. I needed to allow for the tiny strides of the little one next to me. My hand came out of my pocket and reached down to grasp the tiny upheld hand. Making my way at the speed of a child opened me up to the world around me in a way that was no longer under my control. I was set upon by the environment in a way I would have never allowed without a child.

"Daddy, why's that man eating out of that garbage can?"

"Daddy, why's that lady yelling to herself?"

"Daddy, why's that mommy being mean to her daughter?"

My head whirled as I tried to take in the sights and sounds that I otherwise would have blocked out. I looked over my shoulder to the outdoor seating of a cafe we had just passed where a woman and a young girl were seated. I watched as the woman, who was disheveled and seemingly close to tears, shook her fist angrily at the girl. On the ground around them were several broken crayons, and what looked to be most of a meal from the kid's menu.

Rather than paying attention to her mom, the young girl scowled back at me.

I kept walking, glancing down at my imaginary son next me. "She might not be mean. She might just be frustrated." I said.

"At what?"

I glanced quickly back at the mess on the ground under the table.

"I'm sure I'll find out soon enough."

"What's that supposed to mean?" my imaginary son asked.

"Just that I'm sure being a parent is a lot more stressful and complicated than I can imagine.

"You're imagining me, and I'm pretty chill."

"All I'm saying is that maybe that mom has a good reason for being so mad." I said with earnestness.

"You better not ever yell at me like that," he said.

"Well, you better not ever give me a reason to yell at you like that." I smiled, and an overwhelming sense of tranquility came over me.

"So is this what it's going to be like?" he asked.

"What what's going to be like?"

"You and me."

"I really have no idea," I said.

I thought more about the questions I'd either have to answer or dodge. It made my head hurt.

"What's a Jihadist?"

"What's a child molester?"

"What's cancer?"

I thought about the damage that could be done by exposing a child to the horrors of the world at too young an age. I don't want him to grow up any quicker than necessary. On the other hand, I don't want to shelter him for too long, robbing him of the ability to relate to those around him.

I was going to be a father.

I was going to be a father.

I was going to have to answer questions for someone who would understand the world even less than I did. Was I ready, or even competent enough, for that responsibility? I thought about the reasons I had wanted to delay further our having a child. I had wanted to have a job I was proud of, and now I did. What else? I think that was it. That was the one thing that had always eluded me, and I had found it. But I'm not ready. I've never held a baby before; I wouldn't even know what to do with one. I don't even remember being close to a baby before. The realization came to me that perhaps you're never ready, or more specifically, you never know that you're actually ready until you're in the situation you've been avoiding. It would be such an unprecedented change to our lives that the only way to prepare would be on-the-job training.

We were going to have a baby.

I was going to be a father.

CHAPTER THREE

My Favorite Lie

I lie a lot. Occasionally because I can't bear the consequences of telling the truth, but mostly because I believe in the nobility of the lie. If you can make someone feel good by curtailing the truth, then aren't you doing something good?

This is an issue on which Angie and I do not see eye to eye. Perhaps it's the physician in her that believes the blunt, honest truth is always best for all parties concerned. *You're going to die a horrible, painful, blistering, blotchy, pus-filled death. And by the way, your mascara looks ridiculous.* I, on the other hand, believe that when a person's feelings are concerned, the bigger the whopper the better.

After a few months of employment at Gleeful Meadows, my enthusiasm had been rewarded by a promotion to activities director. I sat in a circle with a group of seniors as I led the morning exercises— stretches while seated (better known as sit-ercises). Then we kicked around a ball. After that, I read stories from Reader's Digest. And then we chatted while sipping coffee.

Cora, who was blind in one eye after having been beaten by her husband forty years earlier, poked me in the side of the neck.

I turned to her. "Why'd you do that?" I asked.

"You're not paying attention."

"Sorry, I've just got a lot on my mind."

"So do I, but you don't see me drifting in and out during your stories."

"You know, that reminds me of when my son, Rick, was born," Iris said. "They came and gave him to me, and I said, 'That ain't my baby.' They told me that, of course he is, and I don't recognize him because they cleaned him all up. But I knew my baby. He had marks on his head from when they used the clamps to get him out. But this baby didn't have any. Then, when we got home, we get a call, and it's the hospital telling us that they gave us the wrong baby. I told them that I tried to tell them that before. So, we took him back, and they give us the one with the marks on his head."

"I wonder how many times that happened that they never knew about," Adeline said.

"Oh, goodness me," Cora said. "I don't even want to think of anything so awful."

It was then that Fred R came into the circle and sat down with us. "Am I in time for exercises?"

"We finished them ages ago," Bernice L said. "What's the matter with you?"

Hazel P, who had a perpetual grimace, even when she smiled, turned to Grace S. "I don't know about you, but I can't hear a darn thing."

Grace was asleep and, therefore, couldn't hear a darn thing either. Hazel pushed herself to her feet, grabbed her walker, and started away from us.

"Hazel," I yelled. She continued on. I stood and ran up to her. "HAZEL, TURN ON YOUR HEARING AIDS."

She smiled and reached into her ears. "Oh, that's better." She continued out the door.

I went back and sat in the circle. As I did, Bernice said about Hazel, "I don't like it when that lady with the big fat feet deadheads the flowers around here, because she leaves a mess everywhere she goes. If someone doesn't tell her to stop, I'm going to give her a piece of my mind."

Hazel's "big fat feet" were a result of swelling from poor circulation that resulted in her having to wear specially designed wraps that protected the bottoms of her feet while she walked. The sight of her swollen toes always made me wince and, depending upon the time of day, to completely lose my appetite.

Cora poked me in the neck again. "Elsie's on about her room again," she said.

I turned my attention to Elsie S, who was talking to the caregiver who had just wheeled another resident into the circle. "They moved me out of my room because the plumbing beneath the floor ruptured," Elsie said. She had actually been moved to another room while her carpet was cleaned, because she refused to wear her adult diaper to bed, and she had finally soaked through her mattress into the carpet. She would later recount the story as: "Someone kept coming into my room at night to pee on the floor." And then: "They hosed down my carpet while I was at bingo, because they wanted me out of that room so someone else could have it." And finally: "I had to change rooms because my previous one exploded."

"Poor Elsie," Cora said. "I'm not so sure she knows one direction from another." Earlier in the week Elsie had said the exact same thing about Cora.

At one hundred and two years of age, Elsie looked like a Care Bear that had been left in the spin cycle for far too long.

By this point, Fred had gotten up and walked to the window. I ignored Cora as she started gossiping about one of the other residents whom she was sure had once cheated at bingo and whom she was waiting for the exact right moment to confront.

I got up and walked to Fred, who was peering out between the window blinds. "Hey there," I said. "What are you looking for?"

"My daughter, Sue, is going to come meet me. I don't want to miss her."

"If you're not in your room, she'll know to find you here."

"I'm worried she might not. I haven't seen her for a few days, and I don't want to take the chance that she'd come and not find me."

"I can call the front desk and let them know to call us here in the activity room as soon as they see her."

Fred shook his head. "I just don't know."

"Why don't you come back into the circle? I'll fix you some hot chocolate."

"I don't think so. Perhaps another time." He opened the door and walked out. I watched him as he walked to the end of the sidewalk and stood there.

"I worry about him," a voice from behind me said. I turned to see Dorothea, hunched over her walker. Dorothea was so thin that if she sat on anything without first putting down her special cushion, she needed pain medication before she could even attempt getting back up on her feet.

Dorothea's husband had passed away twelve years earlier from complications related to his Alzheimer's disease. Like many with the disease, he had stopped eating. When assisted, he would resist. When forced, he would become violent. Dorothea had felt a sense of relief when he died. This was understandable, common, and forgivable.

If such a thing even required forgiveness.

What Dorothea had been forgiven for, and for which she sought absolution, was the way she had treated her husband in the final months of his life. She didn't understand what was happening to him, and so, in her opinion, she had been cruel to him.

"Oh, goodness, Kevin. I was so awful," she had once said. "There was this time that he was convinced there were rats running all over the walls. He was so afraid. I yelled at him to stop his nonsense. I just didn't understand."

"It wasn't your fault," I told her. Not just to sooth her guilt, but because I really meant it.

"It was. I should have been more understanding. I just didn't know what was happening to him."

"That's exactly the point. How could you know how to respond? You didn't understand his disease. You did the best you could with what you knew."

"Some of the things I said were unforgivable."

"I know you, Dorothea. You're not cruel. We all say things that we don't mean when we're tired or afraid."

"That's what my pastor said."

"So, my advice might actually be good?"

"Oh, you're so silly."

"Maybe, but I'm also right about this. Don't punish yourself anymore, Dorothea. Please. You don't deserve it. I'm your friend, and I care about you."

Dorothea stared out the window at Fred. She had felt a kinship with him because of her experience with her husband. She saw the strength of character in him that remained, despite his loss of understanding about the world around him. She was a kind and gentle woman, but toward Fred, even more so. She saw him as her chance to atone for the way she had been toward her husband.

We both watched Fred pacing at the end of the sidewalk, waiting for a daughter who would never come.

That afternoon I took a group of residents to the butterfly dome at the Science Center in downtown Seattle. I had been dreading the outing because of the parking and traffic difficulties I would face in the Gleeful Meadows bus. When we finally arrived, I parked the bus in a No Parking zone and hoped for the best. Seniors were admitted free at the dome, and I snuck along close and didn't pay either. After all, I wasn't the one who wanted to see the butterflies, I was just the chaperone.

Once inside the building, I felt as though I had been charged with the arduous task of keeping ants in a single line at a picnic where food had been scattered everywhere. We had to fight our way through four hundred and eighty-six separate distractions, each with blinking lights, moving parts, and whizzing noises designed to snatch the attention of the members of my group away from our singular goal of witnessing the butterflies. Kids raced around us as we made our way through the building to the elevators, (apparently, I had parked as far as possible from the correct entrance). Selma T was our first casualty. Selma was the tallest senior I had ever met. Hunched over her walker, she stood at six foot one, and I had no idea how tall she had been before osteoporosis had turned her into a question mark. She told me she couldn't go any further and urged us to leave her behind. I got an office chair from a staff member, sat Selma in it, and we continued our death march as I wheeled her in front of me. Ken P, who was always on the verge of falling asleep, began to use the wall for support, and the further we went, the more he resembled someone on a bender at closing time. "I'm fine," he kept saying, while swatting away anyone who came to offer him assistance.

The butterfly dome was more amazing than I ever would have imagined, and if I hadn't been so concerned about losing one of my flock, having one make a scene, or having a bowel blowout, I might have actually enjoyed myself.

"I'm going to eat one if it lands on me," Cora whispered as she walked past me, her face turned to the greenery and blurs of flapping multicolored Rorschach blotches above us.

I couldn't get Fred out of my mind.

"How does your father's Alzheimer's exhibit itself?"

This was a question I often asked people outside of work, in my personal life (the real world outside of the microcosm of seniors and senior-related illnesses), when first hearing of the diagnosis of the loved one of a friend. The question, nearly always, was met with confusion. "They have trouble with their memory, of course. What did you think?" I never responded flippantly to their flippantness, because I knew that, to them, Alzheimer's had a formula laid out step by step by the authors of cinema. First came trouble remembering events and appointments. Then came trouble remembering loved ones. Then came some moment from the afflicted individual's life which they would relive over and over until they died.

Only when one spent significant time around several people with Alzheimer's did it become clear that there was no formula, no map, no traceable route that led through beaten fields. All the fields were different, with unknown crops that bore no similarity in taste or texture, but only held likeness in the simple fact that they must, indeed, one day die.

Of all the people suffering from Alzheimer's whom I've met and become friends with, Fred is surely the one who haunts me the most when I lay awake at night waiting for sleep to come. Fred had the misfortune of being entirely aware of the disease destroying his brain. He knew he could not remember his children. He knew he didn't know where he was most of the time or what he was doing. Most people were spared the indignity of intimate awareness of their loss of self. However, Fred was not that lucky.

DEMENTED ROGUE'S GALLERY

Viola M was the ideal Alzheimer's sufferer. The kind that we all hope we would be if afflicted with the disease. She was oblivious to her illness and lived in a fantasy world in which she was a valued employee of Gleeful Meadows Assisted Living. If you were to follow her around for a day, you would see her looking out windows, staring at the floor, talking to plants as frequently as she did people, and watching every variation of *Law & Order* that she could find by rapid channel surfing. On the other hand, if you were to ask her what she did on that very same day, she would recount doing ten loads of laundry, administering medications, and bathing, showering, and feeding the residents. "Oh, those poor, sick people," she would say, thankfully unaware that she was one of those sick individuals.

Some days she would scold employees whom she thought were lower than her on the totem pole, and other days she would commend those very same employees for the fine job they were doing, telling them that she would keep them in mind the next time she was considering anyone for a promotion. She once disciplined me for chewing gum while on the job and told me, the next time she saw my mouth smacking away, she would send me home without pay. She once told a visiting family member that their father had been taken away by strange men in the middle of the night and told another that they could not visit their mother at this time as the ceiling in her room was on fire. "But please feel free to take a breath mint from the bowl on the front desk next to the flowerpot on your way out."

Whimsy aside, Viola was nonetheless sick, and her family, like so many others, had to adjust to the reality that this woman was not the mom and grandmom they had known all their lives. However, the blessing (it is all relative) in the case of Viola is that her reality of her employment kept her mind and body active, and for this she was happy.

Then there are those with wildly exaggerated emotions. Whether they are deftly aware of their illness or not, they laugh or cry or shout profanities or try to kiss everyone they see. Within a twenty-minute period, Henrietta M punched me in the face, saying that I reminded her of someone she once knew, and then kissed me on the cheek, saying that I reminded her of someone else she once knew. Fortunately, much of the wild mood swings can be controlled by medications, but there always will be the occasional laughing or crying fit, or a fire extinguisher to the side of the head.

Ada H, whose dementia was caused by brain damage from years of alcohol abuse, would steal other people's belongings from their rooms, then destroy the stolen items by either smashing them against a wall or eating them. After realizing what she had done, she would spend the rest of the day crying over the pieces that could never be put back together.

Matthew M's fits of rage (the fire extinguisher to the head incident) appeared not to be connected to current frustrations regarding his situation, nor resurfacing frustrations from the past, but instead from an internal reality that his mind was forcing out into the world around him. Much like Dorothea's husband's visions of rats, and a dog that supposedly followed Frances T everywhere she went, Matthew had become convinced that every person he crossed paths with had some nefarious intention toward him.

There are those who are so detached from the world around them that they appear like the walking dead. They can move about the world, interacting with objects, flicking light switches repeatedly, or constantly rearranging furniture, yet, at the same time, seem entirely unaware of the people around them. Wave your hand in front of their face, and their eyes won't even focus. Opal C, who was always on the move, attempting to escape from the facility, would sometimes walk into you as though she existed on some other plane of existence in which she was a captive in an automated facility in a world where she was the last human alive.

This is the group that frightens family members and new staff the most, as their behavior seems the furthest removed from what we remember of the person we knew or would expect to see in a public forum.

In an environment like assisted living, you have those who can no longer control their bodily functions, and then those who have lost the social training and inhibition that would otherwise keep such things private. Like Len A, who squatted and pooped on the floor in the center of the dining room. His wife had finally sought out a place to take care of him after he did the same thing in the living room at a friend's house, during a dinner party. Public masturbation is also another act that one may encounter. Due to the extraordinarily private nature of sexuality, especially masturbation, this act is the one, above all others, which seems to elicit the greatest shame from the family members of the individual with Alzheimer's.

On the other hand, not all public bathroom breaks are caused by involuntary lack of mental or bodily restraint. When one's history is wiped from their memory, left behind, deep within their subconscious, are the remnants of acts from the past which they no longer remember or associate with the world around them. A man might poop into a flowerpot, knowing that such an act is meant to be undertaken in a receptacle somewhat resembling the flowerpot. Peeing into garbage bins is another popular result when Alzheimer's and bodily functions collide. Alzheimer's disease has a cruel sense of humor. It doesn't take your dignity away from you in the same way other diseases do before they take your life. You don't merely stare from a distance as if in a darkened theater of a cruel play. Alzheimer's forces you to be an active participant in purging yourself of dignity, forcing words into your mouth and actions into your limbs.

For me, the most unsettling group of our Alzheimer's rogue's gallery are those who are aware of their decline. Or, at the very least, aware enough that they feel they are being imprisoned or abandoned by their families for having a disease due to no fault of their own. These folks are prone to severe depression, escape attempts, and even a greater risk of suicide.

Fred was a member of this unfortunate alumni. He was sixty-seven years old, tall and handsome with a Jimmy Stewart quality about him. Two months earlier he had merely had trouble remembering names and dates. Now, the world around him was a constantly shifting jigsaw without any familiar points of reference to hold onto.

"Keep that man away from me," Ariel screamed as Fred came back into the building.

As we tried to calm Ariel down in a chair in the front lobby, his hands shook violently, spilling lukewarm sugar-free cocoa on his lap. "If I see him in my room again, I'm calling the cops."

"What's wrong?" Paul asked as he came out of his office. Paul looked like a Great Dane standing on its hind legs. Shockingly thin, with jowls that gave him the appearance of terminal sadness, Paul was the manager of Gleeful Meadows, though, unfortunately, he spent more time posturing than actually managing.

"He came into my room again last night," Ariel said. "Nearly scared the life right out of me."

"Who?" Paul asked, while surreptitiously checking his watch.

"Fred," I said.

"Why don't you lock your door?" someone asked from elsewhere in the room.

"That's not the point," Ariel said. "The point is that I open my eyes at two in the morning, and he's standing over me, looking down on me with his nobody-home stare."

"It was just a mistake," I said.

"I don't want to hear the Alzheimer's excuse. I hear it all the time." Ariel sipped his beverage and closed his eyes as though it were a calming gulp of whiskey.

"It's not an excuse."

Ariel looked at me through weary eyes. "Discipline is what he needs."

"It's not that simple."

"I've got diabetes, had it since I was a kid. But I'm still alive and productive, because I've got discipline. Discipline in life is what it takes."

"It's not the same thing. Not all diseases can be managed like yours," Paul said.

"Rubbish. Rubbish and earwax."

"What about cancer?" I offered.

"What about it?"

"A person with cancer can't control how quickly or slowly it progresses."

Ariel appeared to ponder this. "They can with medication and treatment," he then said.

"They can *hope* to. But it doesn't always work. Look at Fred that way. He's fighting as well as he can, but he's losing, and it's not his fault."

Later that day, I sat in my office going through my voice messages. As a general rule, our concierge puts all callers directly into my voicemail if they don't ask for me by name, which usually means they're either looking for a gig or pitching their wares, and I have poor sales resistance and don't like to be put on the spot.

Entertainers who cater to assisted living and nursing facilities are an eclectic bunch. There are a few genuine talents and a whole lot of mediocrity. Singers and musicians galore, and then other strange stuff that can't quite be categorized. For example, the laughter lady.

"Hi, it's me, Angela, again. The laughter lady. Haven't heard—" I hit the delete button. The laughter lady led people in laughter therapy (huh? you say). When she had first called to schedule a laughter session with our residents, she said the magic word that all activities directors long to hear: "volunteer." I fit her into every opening in our calendar that I could find. Then she came, and Hazel voiced what we were all thinking, "What is this crap?" Did she tell jokes? No. The room cleared out as she led us in rhythmic chanting of hahaha heeheehee hohoho, and countless other variations of fake laughter.

Like many senior care facilities, Gleeful Meadows had a section that specialized in memory care called the Family Circle. The Family Circle was, in fact, a circle. There was a round, central hallway that served two purposes. The first was that it made the exit much harder for the demented to locate. It could only be entered and exited by electronic pass code and was for residents whose dementia either made them a constant flight risk or unable to integrate with the other residents in assisted living. The majority of the residents in assisted living had some degree of dementia, but it was more of the "I can't remember where my room is" variety as opposed to the "I'm going to take a poop on the kitchen floor" kind.

Exit seeking was common amongst this demographic, and so anything that could be done to minimize the possibility of flight was a definite plus. The other purpose was so that when the exit seekers asked someone where the exit was, they could just point down the hall and say, "That way." This was great, because, technically, they weren't lying, and the residents got a great workout as they walked in circles through the building's single hallway looking for the way out. Eventually, they would forget that they were trying to escape, only to remember later, and, once again, ask where the exit was.

The center of the Family Circle opened up into a courtyard, which saw just as much foot traffic as the circular hallway.

The exit seekers made the Family Circle a busy and fascinating place.

There were the ones who staked out the door and tried to leave when someone else either left or entered. You'd just have to close the door quickly or tell them that you didn't know the code but would go find someone who did.

There were the ones who tried to crack the pass code and would spend hours keying in digits, even though the pass code was actually just the room number that was emblazoned on the exit door.

There were also the panel pushers who would get up on chairs and try to escape through the ceiling paneling.

Then, there were the instigators, like Henrietta and Ada, who would try to rally other residents. "We're prisoners here. This is just a concentration camp for old people. They can't keep us here if we rise up against them." The trouble with this was that residents with dementia are often very impressionable and can get swept up easily by other people's moods and sentiment. Similarly, the good thing about this is that residents with dementia are often very impressionable and can get swept up easily by other people's moods and sentiment—making it easier to quell their uprising with the promise of ice cream or by merely doing a funny dance.

Following the laughing lady's first visit to the community, Paul called me into his office and told me that he never wanted to see her in our building again. On her subsequent visits, I relegated her as far into the Family Circle as possible without her again getting closer to the main building. This kept her out of Paul's sight and gave her a captive audience, most of whom were already perpetually laughing. When we got to the end of her bookings, I didn't have the heart to fire her, so I did the next best thing. I avoided her and let my voicemail do the talking. I continued listening to my messages.

"Kevin, it's Adeline. When can we get the accordion man back?"

"Hi, my name is Mark, I play a kazoo with my nose."

"I need to do community service for a DUI conviction."

"I'm a mime. Yes, I have a voice."

"Kevin, it's Adeline again. When can we go back to IHOP?"

"It's Brownie troop 4838."

"It's Brownie troop 2934."

"It's Angela, the laughter la—"

"Yeah, I'm on work release from prison, and I need to do community service."

"Kevin, It's Adeline."

"My name is Gregor, I play the accordion."

"My name is Michael, I play the accordion."

"My name is Alphonse, I play the accordion."

"…yes, hello? My name is Fred. I found this business card on my nightstand. I don't know exactly where I am, but I know that I need to speak to my daughter. She may be looking for me. I was hoping you might know who I am or who my daughter is. I'd appreciate your help. Well, thank you." The call ended. I looked at my watch. The call had come in about twenty minutes earlier.

When I got to Fred's room, he was already gone. I walked along the hallway, away from the main entrance of the building, looking for him out the windows. From the second floor, there was a wonderful view of the wetlands behind the building and part of the walking path that encircled us. I saw Iris, Marcia B, and Betsie T sitting upon a park bench engaged in conversation.

As I continued down the hallway, the air became rich with the smell of poop. There were no potted plants to conceal the source of the smell in the hall, so it had to come from one of the nearby rooms. I inhaled deeply like a hound in search of quarry. The smell became more intense as I approached the room of Ken P.

I knocked. I knocked louder. As I again raised my fist, Ken opened the door, greeting me with a smile and a fecal waft. One side of his suspenders was caked in poop.

"Hi, Kevin. What can I do for you?" he asked with a mirthful grin.

"I'm looking for Fred," I said. The most likely cause of the smear on Ken's suspenders was that he had rolled them off of his shoulders to use the toilet. He must have somehow managed to sit upon one of the suspender straps with it hanging into the bowl. He seemed unaware of the smell, and I didn't currently have the time to bring it to his attention.

"Fred, eh? Can't say I've seen him since breakfast. Came in wearing his pajamas. Not the sort of attire a gentleman wears out to breakfast."

After requesting a "brown alert" clean up to room 264, I walked back down the hall toward Fred's room. His door was now open. I looked in and saw him standing in the center of the room, looking away from me.

"Fred?" I said.

He turned and looked at me. "Hi there," he said.

"Can I come in?"

"Sure thing," he said before turning his attention back to the window.

I walked in and closed his door. "What are you up to?"

"I'm waiting for my daughter."

"She called and said she wouldn't be in until later. She wants you to relax and said she'd come find you after dinner." These sorts of lies were useful sometimes to help calm an agitated demented resident, or one who had become fixated upon waiting for an imaginary event. They would usually resume the activity after some time, although it did usually give them, and us, a short reprieve.

"I need to talk to her," he said. "I need to know everything is alright."

"She's fine. Everything is alright."

"I need to know." He turned away from me. "I don't remember what she looks like. I don't remember seeing her." He looked back at me. "Why do I know these memories are missing? Why aren't they just gone? Why do I have to be so aware?"

I sat on the edge of Fred's bed. "I don't know, Fred."

After the second ring, Fred's daughter, Sue answered the phone. "Hello?" she said.

"Hi, this is Kevin calling from Gleeful Meadows."

"Oh, my goodness, is everything alright with my dad?" Her voice was filled with panic. This was the usual response I received when calling a family member of one of our residents.

"Everything is fine. I'm just sitting here with your dad, and he wanted to talk to you."

"Is he wondering if I'm alright?"

I looked up at Fred. "Yes."

"This is the fourth or fifth time this week that he's had someone from there call to check on me."

"I'm sorry, I didn't know that."

"Apparently, he always thinks that I'm coming there to meet him."

"That's right," I said.

"One of the night staff called me last evening. She said he was pacing the halls looking for me. It's become too hard for me to look out for him. I'm the only family he has out here. It's too hard for me to do alone."

"I know," I offered without truly knowing how she felt.

"I've decided to move him back to Arizona," she continued. "We have lots of family there who he can be with. I don't know how much time he has left, and I want him to be as happy as possible. That can't happen out here. Here, I'm all he has. I'll talk to him so that he knows I'm okay. Don't say anything about the move. It'll just give him something else to obsess over."

The week leading up to Fred's departure was one of increased anxiety throughout the community. Even though Fred didn't yet know he would be moving, he seemed to sense that there were things left unsaid in the way we looked at or addressed him. He had another altercation with Ariel, which began with Ariel telling Fred to stay on his own side of the dining room, and ended with Fred throwing Ariel to the floor. Luckily, the altercation concluded with nothing more than a bruised rear. The tension between the two of them was something that upset even the other residents, who knew and cared for both men. The irony about their conflict was that Ariel had his own unhealthy dose of Alzheimer's eating away at his mind.

It was not uncommon to find walkers, canes, or even wheelchairs left behind in the activity room following an activity. People who spent their entire lives healthy and vibrant sometimes needed to be reminded that they were no longer such. Usually, I'd catch the resident who had forgotten their mobility aid before they'd strayed too far from my sight. Sometimes, however, they'd slip away like a fiend in the night, and I'd be left like a valet with an unclaimed jalopy. If there was no name on the forgotten item, I'd have to go from room to room of those who may have left it. The most common culprit was Marcia who, regardless of the extraordinary pain she felt from her arthritis and the fragility caused by osteoporosis, almost always forgot that she needed a walker to get anywhere.

On this particular day, Iris and Betsie had each grabbed an arm and were dragging Marcia between them down the hallway to the dining room. I rushed to grab her walker and called after them, though none heard me.

"Sometimes I wonder if those three share one brain between them," Ken said as I passed him.

"That's not very nice," I said over my shoulder.

"Just calling it the way I see it."

I caught up with them and placed the walker in front of Marcia.

"We was wondering why she couldn't get up," Iris said.

"My legs hurt like toothaches," Marcia said, as I helped her up and placed her in the cushioned seat between the handholds of her walker.

"Today you get a free ride," I said as I began to push her, with Iris and Betsie putting their hands on the sides of the handles to help push.

"I'm so feeble," Marcia said. "I hate myself."

"Don't say that. We all need help sometimes."

"Nobody needs as much help as I do."

"There are lots of people who need even more help."

"You're just saying that."

"No, I'm not." As we walked to the dining room, I thought about what Ken had said about these three. They all lived in regular assisted living, though they each had one foot in the Family Circle and the other foot on a roller skate. They were three of the first friends I had made when I began working at Gleeful Meadows, and I had watched their minds deteriorate on a daily basis. Thankfully, they had deteriorated at roughly the same rate so that none of them got frustrated or angry at the others.

Their memories were now so bad that they could ask me what and when the next activity was, take two steps away, and then turn back to me as though the conversation had never taken place. Repeating conversations like that can take getting used to, as well as demand a great deal of patience. I had taken to writing activity reminders on Post-it notes and giving them to "The Three Musketeers" each time they approached me. Upon cleaning Betsie's room, the cleaning staff would find dozens of Post-it notes, many of which with the exact same information on them.

What bothered me most about the flippantness and lack of sensitivity of Ken's remark was the knowledge his own wife had once been like these three. Though the destruction of her mind from Alzheimer's had happened long before. She was a resident of ours who lived in the Family Circle. Ken would visit her nearly every day. Sometimes I would see him outside her room, not willing, or able, to take those last few steps to see her, and then turn around and leave.

I don't know if his attitude toward Marcia, Iris, and Betsie was a defense mechanism to protect him against his own pain. Or perhaps he was just a bully at heart.

"What's going on here?" I asked Ariel and Fred as I walked up to them sitting upon a park bench in the courtyard. They each had an arm over the other's shoulder and a paper cup in their other hands.

"Enjoying the afternoon with a good friend and a bit of whisky," Fred said.

"Good friends, eh?" I said.

"We get by," Ariel said, giving me a wink. Later that day, I ran into Ariel, and he told me that life was too short to hold grudges, and besides, how could he keep a feud going with a man who couldn't even remember that they were supposedly adversaries.

I suppose sometimes even Alzheimer's can be a beautiful thing.

The day of Fred's move arrived and began with Fred's daughter telling him that he was, in fact, moving. He then came and joined us for morning exercises while his belongings were packed and moved from his room. Ken fell asleep during the exercises and then plopped out of his chair onto the floor. Fred and I helped him to his feet while the ladies looked on. Instead of going back to his room, Ken sat back down and quickly resumed his nap.

I asked the group to share memories of their favorite moments with Fred.

"There was that time when he told that door-to-door nuisance of a salesman where to go," Molly G said. This, of course, had never happened, but Fred wouldn't remember one way or another.

"I remember the day he first came to live here. I went up and introduced myself as his neighbor," Dorothea said, tears welling up in her eyes.

"I remember he sits next to me at lunch time," Grace said. "That's about it."

"My fondest memory with Fred was when we went for a walk after supper one day and saw a deer come into the courtyard," Ethel C said.

I remembered that day as well. Bea F had called me up at the front desk to tell me about the deer. I had run outside with a camera, leaving my desk and the ringing phone, and captured a photo of the deer before it had bounded back into the woods behind the community.

It seemed like a long time ago. It was a different season, and I had only been working at Gleeful Meadows for a few weeks at the time. I hadn't yet fallen in love with my job, still acclimatizing to the unexpected quirks of the environment, and was preparing myself to give my notice. Then I met Fred. He came to the front desk to introduce himself, and we talked about the pleasure the deer sighting had brought us. He was one of the few residents in the community who had grown up in a city, and therefore, seeing wildlife was as exciting to him as it was to me.

I uploaded the photograph of the deer from my digital camera onto the screen of my computer for Fred to see. He then told me of his experiences during World War II as a photographer for the air force. I enjoyed that first encounter with Fred, and it stood as a realization to me that the residents could be much more than work. They could be my friends.

As I was locking up the reception lounge that day, Fred knocked on the door just as I was about to turn out the lights. He had brought with him a book of photographs which he had taken during the war. We spent the next two hours going through the book together, with Fred describing the details and events surrounding each of the photos. His memory was impeccable. Or so it had seemed at the time.

As dusk settled, Fred and I sat in the foyer of the reception lounge, each sipping a cup of hot cocoa, while his daughter and son-in-law finished loading Fred's belongings into their car.

"How many times have we sat like this?" Fred asked.

"Not nearly enough," I said.

He sipped his cocoa. "I never could have imagined this would be how I'd spend my golden years." He was silent for quite some time, before finally continuing. "If you had come to me twenty years ago, or even five years ago, and told me that I'd waste away and not even be able to remember my children's names, I would never have believed it possible. Life sure does throw strange and horrible surprises at us. It's like my mind isn't my own."

"There are lots of people here who are going to miss you," I said.

"I won't miss them. I already don't remember them."

"Dorothea's quite fond of you. She says you remind her of her husband."

"I'm sorry, but I don't even know who Dorothea is."

There was nothing I could say, so I just sipped my cocoa.

An hour later, Fred was gone from our lives forever. This last conversation with him was one I knew I would keep with me forever, and yet I knew he had already forgotten it. His family had come to collect him and his things, and, hopefully, as he began the rest of his life in Arizona, some of the time he had spent with his daughter Sue and her family would stay with him.

"Excuse me," a small voice said.

I turned and saw a young girl in the front entrance with an enormous collection of helium balloons. The largest and highest read *Happy Birthday Grandpa.*

"You must be Jessica," I said. She smiled. "Your Grandpa Fred spoke of you often." Her smile widened. In reality, I had read her name in Fred's profile.

"We couldn't fit the balloons in the car. Is it alright if I leave them here?"

I nodded. "Of course."

After the second knock, I heard Dorothea's voice beckoning me into her room. I opened the door and went in. She was reclined in a comfy-looking chair watching *The Price is Right.*

"My goodness, what is all that?" she asked.

"They're the balloons that Fred's family gave him for his birthday. He knew he couldn't take them with him, and since your birthday was so close to his, he asked me to give these to you."

Her eyes welled and reddened, tears pouring down her cheeks. "Praise the Lord," she said. She reached out and touched one of the balloons. "From Fred?" She now openly wept, putting her face in her hands. After some time, she looked up at me. "This is the most wonderful birthday gift I've ever gotten. Fred is so special to me, because he reminds me of my husband. It's like my husband has forgiven me for the way I treated him. Oh, praise the Lord."

Tears came to my eyes as well.

CHAPTER FOUR

Answers in the Trash

Our newest resident was Pennsylvania Dutch, Millicent L. That's precisely the way she introduced herself to everybody. She moved from another assisted living facility, where we were told they could not provide the level of care she required. Our facility, on the other hand, prided itself on its ability to cope with residents requiring a high level of care. The intake assessment was completed, and the move followed shortly thereafter.

I peered out the window as Millicent and her motorized wheelchair were lowered off of the Cabulance (which is exactly what its name implies). It is part taxicab and part ambulance. I felt a sense of foreboding that I had not been able to shake since I had taken the initial inquiry call from Millicent, which she had made from a geriatric psychiatric ward. We were told that her medications were now under control and that she was good to go. Classic horror movie dialogue uttered right before twenty people are stabbed to death and disemboweled.

As soon as the regal-looking woman's motorized chair touched the ground, she hit the throttle and propelled herself forward at an alarming rate. Eva, our marketing director, had gone out front to greet Millicent and could not get out of the way in time and was knocked off her feet. She fell onto Millicent, who then jerked her chair to the side, sending Eva to the ground. Eva's long black ponytail, which stretched down to her bum, flipped up over her head as she fell. When she started to get to her feet, her hair then dropped off the side of her shoulder and got pressed under her knee, causing her to fall forward once again.

Millicent continued on into the building, where it was my turn to say hello.

"Hi, I'm…"

She continued past me, down the hallway, in the direction of the elevator.

After a moment, I hurried after her. I matched her pace and jogged beside her. "I'm Kevin, the activities director," I said as I wheezed.

"I'd like some hot cocoa," Millicent answered. "With nonfat milk and six small marshmallows."

We reached the elevator and stopped. I was winded. Her chair was not.

"Well, are you going to push the button, or is that not a grand enough activity for you?" she said.

I withdrew my finger like a pistol, and as I stretched it out to the button, I whistled like a bomb dropping toward its mark. BOOM!!! I took sideway glances at Millicent as we waited silently for the elevator to arrive. She clearly took great care with her appearance, but in the sort of way an aging starlet might, who knows, in the back of her mind, that her glory days are more behind than in front of her. The red of her lips and cheeks was just a little too red for her skin tone. Not that I'm a beautician by any means, but she looked like an animated mannequin with a red smear on her teeth and a large bouffant of blonde hair.

Once in her room, Millicent drove a quick lap in a circle then headed into the bathroom. She then drove out of the bathroom backward, clipping the doorframe and sending splinters to the floor. "This room won't do!" she yelled. "I can't live here."

"What's wrong?" Eva asked as she came into the room.

"The view. The view is no good. I can't be expected to look at the freeway all day, every day, until I die." She didn't look at us but continued, instead, to stare out the window at two cars parked along the shoulder of the freeway, which looked to have been in an accident.

"You won't be spending much time in your room. We have lots of fun activities going on all the time that you'll want to attend," Eva said.

"Was that the sales pitch you gave to my son in order to get him to spring for this partial view?"

"I think that, after a night or two, you'll come to love this room."

Millicent ignored Eva and drove full speed toward the closed front door. With a loud thud, she crashed into it, and the rubber bumper on the front of her chair left a dark black stain against the white paint. She reversed, spun 180 degrees so that she was facing us, and then threw herself out of her chair onto the floor.

Seeing the partially paralyzed woman flail on the carpeting in front of us was reminiscent of a fish flipping about inside a boat. We stared in amazement before rushing to her aid.

That was our introduction to Pennsylvania Dutch Millicent.

After a quick conversation between Eva and Paul, it was decided that Millicent's belongings would be moved into another available room with a view more to her liking. An hour after the decision had been made, we finished carrying everything from one room to the other. Satisfied with the view, it was then that Millicent drove into her new restroom and once again yelled, "I can't live here!"

As a result of Millicent's stroke, she was paralyzed on the right side of her body. The wall next to the toilet in the room we had just moved her out of had had a support bar drilled into it that Millicent could grip onto with her left hand. The new room was on the opposite side of the building, and the supporting wall next to the toilet was on the *right* side of the toilet, which would do her no good at all.

We had to move everything back into the first room.

The next morning, Millicent ran her scooter into the outside of the activity room door. Her scooter was equipped with a horn, but that wouldn't allow her to make the entrance that breeding such as hers no doubt deserved. She reversed, then slammed into the glass door once again. One of our care staff ran to assist her and had the door open a crack before Millicent came forward again, slamming the door back

57

against the young caregiver's face. As Millicent reversed, the caregiver recovered and opened the door. Millicent came speeding into the room.

I was thankful for the distraction, as fifteen seniors and I were an agonizing half hour into an activity that turned out more disastrous than I could ever have imagined. It was the first and last time for: Name that Smell!

I had divided everyone into two teams, and one contestant from each team was blindfolded while I held an item up in front of their nose for them to smell. The activity had had a promising start as Grace had correctly identified a banana. As it turned out she was the only one who still had a sense of smell.

That was followed by:

Guesser	Guess	Actually
Sol M	Chocolate	Mustard
Leona P	Chocolate	Gorgonzola Cheese
Elsie S	Chocolate	Soya Sauce
Ken P	Chocolate	Dill Pickle
Adeline S	Chocolate	Pineapple
Iris H	Chocolate	Peanut Butter
Cora D	Chocolate	Hot Sauce
Hazel P	Chocolate	Garlic
Anna P	Gorgonzola Cheese	Chocolate

This thankfully was followed by:
Thump!

We all turned to see Millicent lying face down in the corner of the room. No one would ever accuse her of not knowing how to make a grand entrance or an impression that wouldn't soon be forgotten.

Several of the women shrieked. Millicent attempted to squirm with the half of her body that permitted her to do so. I slapped the emergency buzzer on the wall next to me as I ran over to her. I was joined by Sol M and Ken, who I suppose had been awoken from his nap by either the shrieks or the sound of Millicent's face colliding with the floor.

"Are you alright?" he asked.

"I...I don't know. I hope nothing's broken."

"Just stay there, help is on the way. Isn't it, Kevin?" Ken asked.

I wanted to tell them that this was all an act for attention. That we should just turn our backs on her and go back to our game and let her squirm on the floor behind us. That we were just encouraging her behavior. But, the truth is that we all act out for attention in different ways and for different reasons. Sometimes it's because of a person's feeling of superiority. But, just as often, perhaps even more so, it's because of their feeling of inferiority. Besides, responding to Millicent's need for attention was less painful than continuing to play Name that Smell!

Liv, one of the care staff, emerged and helped me load Millicent back into her chair. Soon after, Sarah, one of the nurses, arrived and gave Millicent a quick once-over. She beamed at the attention of everyone in the room. After she was declared unbroken, I asked her to join our group. She turned on her scooter and manipulated her way into the circle.

"Everyone, this is Millicent," I said.

Marcia suddenly looked up. "Two Millicents?" she asked. "Surely not. I already know another Millicent."

"We have several, actually," I said. "We've got three Bernice's, four Cora's, and six Leona's. We try to get as many residents as possible with the same names to make it easier for us to remember you all."

"That was quite the tumble you took," Cora said.

"Oh, yes. Sometimes my chair gets a mind of its own and bucks me off. Just like a mare I once had named Sally Mae, the Third."

"I used to help my father break the horses we had on our farm," Iris said. "I used to ride them bareback. Even the ones that people said couldn't be rode."

"Well, Sally Mae, the Third, was a lady of the finest stock, who knew how to treat her rider," Millicent said.

"Then how come she threw you?" someone asked.

"She was startled when an unskilled rider came into our line. It was their fault."

On the week that Fred moved out, Tom B moved in. In the memory department, the two men were very much alike, but where the last one was withdrawn, this one was gregarious. He wore enormous glasses with thick, black plastic frames and a crew cut that was in drastic contrast to the pajama bottoms that hung loosely around his waist. He moved about the activities room, perched above his walker, flirting with all the ladies as he introduced himself. He made his way over to me and stuck out a massive paw. I took his hand and shook it as though he and I had not just done so an hour previously. "How do you do? The name's Tom."

"Glad to meet you, Tom. I'm Kevin, the activities director."

"So how do you want to divide these ladies between us? Alphabetically or chronologically?"

"We could always just draw names from a hat," I said as I continued moving chairs into a semicircle.

"What are you setting up for? Should I have bought a ticket for the prom?" he asked.

"Happy hour," I said. "We serve drinks and have a little entertainment."

"What's the entertainment?"

I stopped and reached into my back pocket. "How about you?" I said as I handed him a piece of paper which contained the lyrics to "Shipoopi."

He looked it over. "I'm sure I can fit this in before I get my letter from the president."

"What letter is that?"

"I'm ninety-six. I got four more years to go before I get my letter from the president. Then I'll cash in my chips. Didn't you know that the president writes everyone a personal letter who makes it to a hundred?"

"No, Tom, I did not know that."

"It's true." He looked around the room. "Guess I'm the oldest one around here."

"Actually, not by a long shot. We've got lots of residents in their late nineties. And even one who's over a hundred."

"Surely not."

"It's true." I pointed over to Elsie, who was seated in her wheelchair talking amongst a group of ladies. "Elsie over there is a hundred and two."

"You've got to be joking." He turned his back on me and made his way over to Elsie. "Excuse me. My name's Tom and I just moved in here."

"How do you do?" Elsie said.

Tom pointed to me and said, "The fellow over there is trying to tell me that you're over a hundred."

"That's right, I'm a hundred and two."

"Well, I've got to get me some of whatever you've got, because you look like you could do cartwheels in the rain." Elsie smiled at him. Tom then leaned toward her. "You know, I've always wanted to kiss a hundred-year-old woman. Especially one as good looking as you." He then planted a kiss on her cheek.

A short time later, the happy hour crowd sat with their drinks in hand, snacking on gluten-free, low-sodium chips, and looking toward the front of the activities room at Tom, Iris, and Elsie, who each held a music and lyric sheet in their hands. Tom rested against his walker, Iris stood, and Elsie remained seated in her wheelchair. I pressed Play on the CD player, and the music began. A moment later, Cora began her accompaniment on the piano.

"Hi, I'm calling from Gleeful Meadows Assisted Living," I said into the phone in my office. "One of our residents, who used to live at your facility, lent a flower vase to a friend and would like to come over to pick it up. I was just wondering what a convenient time to receive her would be?"

"Who is the resident?" the woman asked.

"Millicent L."

There was a noticeable pause.

"Hello?" I said.

"We have a restraining order against Millicent. She's not permitted within five hundred feet of our property."

"Excuse me?"

"Any property of hers that she believes is still on our premises will be returned via UPS."

"Are you sure we're talking about the same person?"

"Pennsylvania Dutch?"

Oh crap, I thought.

"Does she have her dog with her?" the woman asked.

"No. What dog?"

"You'll find out. She'll begin a sob story soon enough about how she can't live without her dog, Nibbles. We actually had to evict Nibbles a week before we evicted Millicent. She's called Nibbles for good reason. When she's not being choked to death, or being dragged behind Millicent's scooter with the leash wrapped around one of its wheels, she's eating everything in sight."

Over the next week, Millicent pulled her emergency bedside cord a total of three hundred and twelve times, threw herself onto the floor six times, and yelled at, grabbed, hit, slapped, and/or ran over twelve people.

The chicken was too dry. The salmon was too tough. She wanted Guatemalan coffee beans when we had Kenyan, and Moroccan when all we had was Jamaican. She was a cliché made flesh. She took every corner too tight and too fast and left splinters, ripped wallpaper, dents, torn fabric, and missing paint chips in her wake.

I wondered if, perhaps, we were heading toward some larger disaster which I had helped facilitate. After all, I was the one who had taken the initial inquiry call from Millicent. She had seemed pleasant and gracious, and the only indication that anything was amiss was that she had called from the geriatric psychiatry ward. She said that she had been temporarily committed because of a misunderstanding, and I wondered now if that misunderstanding was entirely on *her* part.

I waved through the activity room window toward Arnold D, who was outside for his morning walk. He glanced in my direction and waved back. Arnold didn't attend many activities, because he was still coping with the death of his wife and, as he put it, "The room full of wrinkles and white hair reminds me too much of her." His visits to the activity room were made even more uncomfortable by the palpable realization that most of the ladies in it looked toward Arnold as the perfect bed warmer. Arnold was tall, distinguished, nearly deaf, and had a sense of humor as dry as a glass of straight gin. He had been a colonel in the air force and had been forced into retirement by a stroke.

One of the qualities that made Arnold so endearing to us all was the self-deprecating nature of his storytelling. For most, self-deprecation comes across as pathetic, a realization that one sees themselves in as poor a light as the world does. But with Arnold, and other great people who are likewise great storytellers, it comes across as a mark of humility. Arnold would much rather tell the stories of his misadventures than those that put the medals on his chest.

My favorite was that of his first flight test, which had been in an open cockpit two-seated biplane (the make and model escapes me). Arnold had been so nervous that he had forgotten to strap himself in. He had performed his required aerial maneuvers flawlessly, that is until he was instructed to perform a loop, at the apex of which he fell out of the plane.

Thank God for parachutes and second chances.

Iris started up as though triggered by a timer or a motion sensor. "I used to help my father break the horses we had on our farm. I used to ride them bareback. Even the ones that people said couldn't be rode."

"You told us that story yesterday," Millicent said. "You're supposed to tell us something about you that we don't know."

"I've only just met you. How could I have already told you my story?"

"You did. Yesterday."

"If you don't want to hear from me then just say so."

Twenty minutes later, we were buried within Iris's contribution to our revelations of what most people didn't know about us. "...then when we got home, we get a call, and it's the hospital telling us that they gave us the wrong baby. I told them that I tried to tell them that before. So, we took him back and they gave us the one with the marks on his head." Millicent L hung on every word, blissfully unaware that this was the first of thirty-six times she would hear the same story, and each telling, according to Iris, would be the first.

The next day, my thoughts were given a temporary reprieve from Millicent as we had another resident move into the community. Her name was Wesley Marie P.

Our feelings toward the people around us, and the situations we find ourselves in, are as out of our ability to control or understand as the actions of others. Our own actions are the rationalization of our feelings, the opaque reflection of the outside world we hold within us. Whom we love, whom we distrust, whom we pity, and the causes we hold dear are decided upon by something deep within us, without our consent.

I don't know what Wesley Marie was like before her Alzheimer's. I rarely know what our residents were like in their lives before assisted living. I know Wesley Marie was a teacher. I know she and her husband had one child and adopted another. I know her husband died shortly after the birth of their daughter. I know she never remarried. That's all I know.

"My father's name was Wesley, my mother's name was Marie, and so they named me Wesley Marie," she had said at our first meeting.

In the short time I knew her, I formed a bond with Wesley Marie that I found difficult to explain. I wondered if it was because I had grown up without grandparents of my own. I later came to doubt that as a factor in my affection toward her. I didn't see her as a grandparent. I saw her as a friend. A very dear friend. I like to believe that she saw me in the same light.

Every morning, Wesley Marie had the same routine. She watered every plant, flower, shrub, and bush on the property, and then went for a Café Americano at Starbucks. Her dementia was already affecting her mental faculties, so her daughter-in-law kept a Starbucks gift card fully loaded for Wesley Marie's caffeine needs.

"We passed a woman out front who seems like she'd be a nice friend for Mom," Lisa, Wesley Marie's daughter-in-law, had said to me after they had finished moving her things in. "That's her there." She pointed out the window.

I looked out the window and saw Doris D scratching her elbow as she walked through the lawn of our courtyard. "Doris threw a plate of food at another resident a couple of weeks ago. She's a bit prickly," I said. I knew I didn't have to say more.

Wesley Marie never spoke to any of the other residents, nor did she participate in any of the activities. She had a polite aversion to the other residents, not a result of snobbery, but more closely resembling the way that fish and trees rarely have much to do with one another.

After Lisa and Wesley Marie walked away to survey the grounds, I noticed Iris looking out the window of the activity room. I walked over to her. Outside the window was a spider web with a dead moth in it. Beyond that, Wesley Marie tended to a pot of flowers while Lisa looked on. Beyond them, a path stretched from our property into a wooded area filled with deer, birds, and the fragrant smells of nature and life.

"Hi, Iris, whatcha doing?"

"Nothing much. Just thinking."

"What about?"

"My home and my car that are probably both now in disrepair."

"I'm sure your son is taking good care of them."

"He might want to, but my daughter-in-law don't care about them. There was squirrels on the roof that used to jump down from my neighbor's tree if he didn't keep it trimmed. Who's going to make sure he keeps it trimmed?"

"We could call Rick," I said.

She turned away from me and looked out the window again. "I don't know his number."

"I could get it for you."

"I don't want to know that he don't care about my house. Or maybe they already sold it for the money." She scratched at her cheek. "Do you know I don't get my mail anymore? How can they do that to a person? That even legal? I bet that daughter-in-law of mine opens and reads it all and has a good laugh at my expense knowing I'm all cooped up in here with nowhere to go."

"What do you mean with nowhere to go? You don't have to give up on the life you've had. We're right around the corner from all sorts of shops and cafés, and there's a lovely park not far from here."

"I can't get there."

"Why not?"

"Because I don't even know where we are. I'm afraid I'll get lost, and people will look at me like I'm some batty old fool."

An hour later, we set out on our walk through the neighborhood. There were ten of us. I had rounded up everyone I knew who would jump at the chance for some exercise, or just to get off property, and whom I also wouldn't have to spend too much time trying to wrangle from distractions along the way. Those of us who were able-bodied each pushed along someone in a wheelchair, and our group stretched back for half a block with folks using canes and walkers. In the end, several did get distracted by the sights and sounds around us.

"Who's that?" Betsie asked, pointing to a man across the street.

"I don't know," I said.

"You don't know him?"

"It's a big town."

She pointed to someone else. "Is that Kevin over there?" Betsie asked.

"I'm Kevin."

"I'm looking for someone named Mavis," Betsie said. "I think she used to work somewhere nearby." Mavis was Betsie's daughter, who came to visit her mom nearly every day and whom Betsie had completely forgotten. The name, however, was continually stuck in Betsie's mind and was forever resurfacing in various reincarnations.

"That's a bigleaf periwinkle," said Wesley Marie as she pointed toward the edge of a nearby garden.

"Really?" I said as I turned to look.

She pointed at another. "That's an Aleutian violet."

"Oh my."

"That's a flower-of-an-hour."

"Did you make that up?"

She kept on walking. I waited at the next corner for the rest of our group to catch up. We had gone in a big circle and were now near the rear of Gleeful Meadows. I saw the faces of Henrietta M, Ada H, and Frances T staring out at us from one of the windows of the Family Circle. Henrietta and I made eye contact, and I waved at her. At first, I thought she was merely waving back. Then I noticed there was more urgency to her gesturing. She was pointing at the base of the windowsill, and then the top. She signaled with both hands and then beckoned me forward. It suddenly occurred to me that she, in fact, didn't recognize me at all, but rather thought that I was a random passerby whom she hoped would help spring her from the locked window which held them captive. She no doubt was currently entwined in some fantasy where she and her friends were hostages or prisoners of one kind or another.

I waved, turned from her, and walked away.

A short time later, my walking group and I sat beneath the canopy of a large elm tree, licking Popsicles we had picked up at Safeway, and laughing at the poor suckers going past us whom we watched hurrying from what seemed like one emergency to another. We talked about our childhoods, something even the most baffled of my ladies could recall, and all laughed at Iris's tale of riding upon the back of a large cow all the way from her own farm to her neighbor's because she had been too lazy to walk.

After a time, Wesley Marie began picking and eating blackberries from a nearby vine, and I inquired whether it was safe to do so. They all laughed at my city-folk ignorance, and I told them that the only fruit I had ever eaten had come from the supermarket. As we all joined in picking and eating the blackberries, the ladies all told me of their experiences growing up on farms. I was the only member of our little group who hadn't been born on a farm and, in fact, had never set foot on one. It was that day that I learned the difference between jelly and jam and that, in their eighties, nineties, and even hundreds, these women were more capable of tackling hardship than I likely would ever be.

"That's a goosefoot violet," Wesley Marie said on our walk back to Gleeful Meadows.

"You sure know your flowers," I said.

"That's a clammy ground cherry."

"Yuck."

"That's a northern blazing star."

"Beautiful."

"That's a long-tube evening primrose."

"That's a dwarf purple monkeyflower."

"That's a curly pondweed."

And my education continued all the way back to our community.

"Take me to the store," Millicent L said as we came in the door. "I need apples and oranges and grapes and candy."

"I can't take you right now, Millicent. We're about to start another activity."

"I have to go now."

"You should have come on our walk. I told you before we left. We went to Safeway."

"My scooter wasn't charged."

"I can take you tomorrow."

"You have to take me now."

"I'm sorry, Millicent, but I can't. You're free to go yourself. Lots of our residents in electric scooters go on their own. It's a great way to maintain some independence."

She blew out a gust of air, threw her chair into gear, and then raced forward toward the front door. I lunged for it, pushing it open just as the front of her chair began to collide with it. She drove down a short ramp off of the sidewalk and onto the parking lot pavement. A car that was entering had to swerve to avoid hitting her. As she passed the car, I heard Millicent honk a horn on the controls of her chair. And then she was gone.

Paul came into the building a few moments later. "I almost crashed into Millicent."

"That would have been cool," Shana, our head nurse, said. Shana was gay, and open and proud about it. Her orientation was perfectly obvious to everyone except for the residents, who were constantly asking her why some gentleman hadn't yet scooped her up off the market.

"Where's she going?" asked Paul.

"The store," I said.

"That's going to be a disaster."

"Probably."

As Eva and I stood at the front desk sipping coffee, Grace walked up to us and handed me a paper bag.

"These are for you," she said.

I took the bag from her and opened it. Inside were half a dozen cookies. "Thank you, Grace. That was so thoughtful."

"They are only for you. Not to share. Just for you. I don't know these others."

"No worries." I turned to Eva. "I don't know them very well either."

"My son brings me the cookies. I don't like the chocolate chip. The chocolate chip makes my knees heavy." We watched as Grace walked away, pushing her walker and dragging her oxygen mask and tank behind her.

"That was so sweet," Shana said.

"Very sweet," Eva agreed as she took the bag from me and tossed it into the garbage.

"Why did you do that?" I asked.

"Poopy fingers," Eva said.

"Poopy fingers," Shana agreed.

"What's poopy fingers?"

"You ever wipe your ass a little too enthusiastically and one of your fingers accidentally tears through the paper, touching your butthole with the dirty business on it?" Shana asked.

"Until now I thought I was the only one," I said.

"Well, imagine that exact thing the next time one of these little old ladies offers you food. Some of them can't remember to bathe. Imagine how many of them can't remember to wash their hands."

I shook my head and left the relative calm behind the front desk, ventured through a hallway and into the activity room where my ladies were sprinkled about the room, engaged in conversations, assembling puzzles, sipping coffee, and staring off into space. The Three Musketeers were seated by the fireplace. Iris was riled up about something, red-faced, with her fists clenched in the air above her head. She had Marcia's undivided attention, who was flanked by Betsie, who was sorting out the collection of tissues and napkins that she had wadded into her purse.

"You ever notice there's not much ever going on around here?" Hazel said to someone off in the corner of the room. "What the heck are we paying these people for if we're just going to sit around all day waiting to die?"

I fixed myself a cup of coffee and sat next to Elsie, who was telling the story of how she got her "bum knee."

"It was when I was in my forties and a bee stung me on the knee. When it did that, it laid its eggs below the skin. The eggs are still in there, but they haven't hatched yet. I have to stay active, otherwise they may decide to hatch, and I'll lose my leg altogether, and the bees'll come out flying all over the place. So far, I've kept them relatively content, and it just gives me trouble sometimes on cold days, but not so bad that I ever had to miss a dance."

I never would have imagined that my best friends would end up being geriatric ladies.

"You're not allowed to sit down, are you?" Cora said as she walked up to me.

"Why can't I?"

"You're supposed to be working."

"I am working. Can you believe it? This is my job." I sipped my coffee with exaggerated gusto.

"I'd sure like to meet your wife," Grace said.

"Why's that?" I asked.

"Because I want to know what sort of a woman would marry a man who acts like a kid."

"I'm only silly with you ladies. When I leave here, I'm serious all the time."

"I don't believe you," Elsie said.

"It's true. My smile is just part of my uniform; it comes off when I get home."

I left the room and went back to the reception desk. "Has Millicent come back from the store yet?" I asked Jennifer, the concierge who had replaced me.

"Haven't seen her," she said with a smile. I stared for a brief moment at Jennifer wondering if, in fact, she even knew who I was talking about. Jennifer interacted with the residents as little as possible, and with the rest of the staff almost as infrequently. I wondered how someone with such a low social IQ could have been hired for a position that required not only constant contact with people, but courteous and professional contact. Paul had a reputation for hiring ladies who were young and beautiful, and Jennifer, by measure of Paul's standards, was neither. Jennifer was in her early fifties and had a tight bun of gray hair, in which she hid a penny she had had since she was five and considered good luck.

"Crap," I said. "Millicent probably went and got herself killed just to spite me." I ran my hands through my hair, genuinely anxious. Millicent had been gone far longer than I had anticipated. It was part of our philosophy to encourage independence in our residents, but I was beginning to believe that Millicent would take any independence we gave her and exploit it. The difficulty with assisted living was that the residents, unless determined a danger to themselves or others and placed in the Family Circle, were free to come and go as they pleased. We had no right to tell them where they could go or what they could do. If Millicent had been hit by a car, or taken advantage of by a scam artist who preyed on the elderly, it wouldn't have been my fault for letting her go out on her own or encouraging her to do so. But that knowledge would not give me reprieve from the guilt I would feel, as though I had been party to a crime or had been a bystander who did nothing but stand in the shadows and watch the innocent be victimized.

It was now raining heavily. It had become one of those rare afternoons where the sun had given up and a premature dusk had settled on the city. Through the fog, I saw the taillights of a pickup truck as it stopped just beyond our front entrance. Two figures emerged from the truck and unloaded something from the back. They then helped a third figure from the truck and lowered them into the object from the back. They began to push it toward the entrance.

I went and opened the door. I then saw that it was Millicent and her chair they were pushing. There was no power to the wheels, and they made a heavy grinding sound as they turned against the gears. Millicent was wet and shivering.

"What happened, Millicent?" I asked.

She didn't answer me. The two who had brought her in were a middle-aged man and woman, who both wore matching baseball caps that read "I'm not with him/her" (respectively). "We found her out along the side of the highway."

"I...I...I got lost. I needed to get...to get some fruit. My doctor says an apple a day, it...it...it keeps the doctor away."

I felt bad for her, as I would for anyone who had been stuck out in the rain, but I had the uneasy feeling that I had been bamboozled. The highway was nowhere near the supermarket, and Millicent was a smart woman who knew her way around town...and also how to elicit maximum sympathy, while at the same time inflicting maximum guilt. "My...My scooter ran out of...it...it ran out of batteries and I didn't know what to do. I couldn't move. I wanted some apples because I... because I want to be healthy."

"I want to speak to someone in charge," the man said.

"You're so kind," Millicent said to them as the woman stroked her hand. "But you don't need to get involved any further…you've already done so much."

I explained to the two about our philosophy of care designed to encourage independence, though, as I looked at Millicent's flushed cheeks and matted wet hair, it sounded more like an excuse than an explanation. Should we not be protecting someone from themselves, even if the harm they do to themselves is meant only as a tool to spite others? Would that have protected either of us that afternoon? I wondered that as Millicent and the man and woman were ushered into Paul's office. Before the door closed behind them, Millicent looked over her shoulder, smiled at me, and winked.

That weekend passed uneventfully. As Angie worked, I watched horror movies and surfed the internet. When I returned to work on Monday morning, I saw Millicent's son-in-law loading the trunk of his car with Millicent's belongings. Paul's office door was closed, and I could hear Millicent sobbing within.

"What's going on?" I asked Jennifer.

"Millicent is being sent out to geropsych."

"You've been listening at the door?"

"Eva can hear everything through the wall in her office. She's been keeping me up to date."

From Eva's office, through the wall, I learned that Millicent had slapped one of the caregivers over the weekend. There was a clause in every resident's contract which allowed us to evict them within thirty days of moving in. However, they first needed to be admitted to a geriatric psychiatric facility to determine whether their current behavior is baseline or caused by a new, unfamiliar situation and could be corrected by either an increase or decrease in medication.

A short time later, after a wheelchair-accessible taxi had taken Millicent away, I sat on a bench outside the front door to the building. At the end of our parking lot was an enormous dumpster. I saw Millicent's son-in-law throwing boxes from his trunk into the bin. I got up and started walking toward him. By the time I reached him, he had finished, closed his trunk, and driven off.

Inside the dumpster were six sealed cardboard boxes. I reached in and tried to pick one of them up; however, it was too heavy for me to pull free without getting any garbage funk on my clothing. I removed my car key from my pocket and used it to cut through the tape holding the box closed. The box was full of a book called *The Sandcastle of Cabo San Lucas* written by Millicent L.

I took a copy out and flipped through it. It was a self-published account of Millicent's life as a carefree socialite living amongst the wealthy in a Mexican seaside resort. There were photographs of her with celebrities, politicians, and royalty. She and her husband had made their fortune in real estate allowing her to quit her job as a schoolteacher and he his job as a pilot. As described in the book, her husband's flying had continued, though now on their own private plane. Their life together was something depicted in cinema and dreams. They thought it would last that way forever.

I thought back to the previous week when I had hooked up a computer to the plasma TV in the activities room to show the residents satellite images on Google Earth. They took turns giving me the addresses of their children and grandchildren, and I showed them what those houses looked like from outer space. They were speechless. I tried to imagine what it was like to see the modern world through their eyes. Things that they never could have imagined would be possible in their lifetime. "We're floating with angels," James F had said.

When it was Millicent's turn, instead of an address, she gave me longitude and latitude coordinates. When we found the location, what little light she had within her seemed to die. I zoomed in as much as I could until it seemed as though we were looking at a postcard of a Mexican beachside.

"This isn't right. It can't be," Millicent had insisted.

"What's wrong?" I asked.

"It's gone. It's all gone." She turned her chair on, spun a hundred and eighty degrees, and then drove from the room. At the time, I couldn't understand why she had become so upset.

What Millicent's memoir didn't chronicle was her husband's death from pancreatic cancer and Millicent's subsequent descent into despair and depression. Then her stroke, which had left her entirely dependent on those around her. She was not a mean woman at heart, but shame and anger do strange things to people. She became so intolerable to be around that her own children had broken off contact with her. Most of her remaining fortune had been spent on live-in caregivers and miracle cures, which did nothing but increase Millicent's feeling of self-loathing and despair.

CHAPTER FIVE

Deck of Cards

As in any work environment, there are good days and bad days. The only difference in assisted living is that every bad day feels like you're trapped within a painting by Dali or a sketch by Escher. This day was a bad one, and it unfolded thus:

I had forgotten my work keys at home. When I arrived at the main building, I found all the entry doors still locked. I walked around to the back entrance, which also was locked. I pressed my face to the glass. One of the lights was on inside. Then I saw Tom B. He pushed his walker over to the reception desk and swiveled the chair whimsically before moving out of eyesight. Residents didn't have access to this part of the building after hours. Had he been locked in here overnight?

I knocked, though he did not respond.

I returned to the front entrance, looking for Tom through all the windows. I pressed my face sideways against the windowpane, craning my neck to the side to see the length of the room inside. Tom was now reading a magazine, seated on a couch next to the electric fireplace, which was turned on. Had it been left on overnight, or had he turned it on? I banged on the glass. Still, he didn't hear me. I crouched down, flipped open the mail slot, and called out to him.

When I stood again and looked toward the fireplace, Tom was gone. I moved from window to window looking for him. Then I saw him making his way toward the rear entrance. I quickly ran around the building, getting there just as the door closed behind the emerging Tom. I grabbed at the handle, but it had already clicked into the locked position.

"Good morning," Tom said to me.

"How did you get in there?"

"What do you mean?"

"The doors are locked. How did you get into the building?"

He turned and looked at the doors behind him. "I don't remember," he said, then walked away.

I had to sit outside in the cold and wait for someone else to come along and rescue me.

I later learned that Tom had been sneaking into the building every morning with the cleaning crew. He liked to pretend that it was his own home, and, for the several hours between the time he entered and when we later did, it was his palatial estate. He even ordered the cleaning staff around, which was just fine with them, since none of them could understand a word he said.

Our morning staff meeting was filled with the same *rah rah* pep rally as usual, the only interesting item being the announcement that during the nightshift, two caregivers were discovered by a resident's family member having sex in one of the empty rooms. After the family member had informed the night supervisor, the two employees were given a verbal warning not to fornicate on company time and property. They would have been fired if it wasn't next to impossible to find graveyard shift workers whom you'd actually feel comfortable having around vulnerable seniors. Copulation notwithstanding. However, the two horny staffers decided to walk off the job, either out of embarrassment or the need to finish what they had started, and Paul had been called in to help cover the shift.

After the meeting, Sarah came up to me. "Have you seen Selma's black eye?" she asked.

"Yeah," I said. "It looks like someone hit her across the face with a frying pan."

"I just want you to know that I'm filing a report, and her son told me that she said you were the one who gave her the black eye."

"Anthony said *I* gave it to her?" I asked.

Sarah took her report from a file folder and read from it. "Kevin backhanded my mom."

"That's crazy," I said.

"Anthony said that that's what Selma told him had happened."

"You can't be serious. You're not going to file that incident report, are you?"

"I have to." She put the report back in her file as though afraid I would try to grab it from her and run away with it.

"Let me talk to Selma first."

"I don't think that's a good idea."

"If you file that report, I'm screwed."

She lowered her gaze. "We both know that Selma is sharp as a tack."

"You're saying you believe this?"

"All I'm saying is there's only so long that I can hold off on sending the report to State. We could get shut down because of this."

"We're not getting any younger," I heard Hazel yell. I turned to see the group waiting for me to start their next activity.

As I walked away from Sarah, I turned back to her. "Don't file that report."

I tried to put the situation regarding Selma out of my mind, though, as expected that was impossible.

Our next activity was Movie Time. The previous week I had shown *Crouching Tiger, Hidden Dragon,* and the residents had loved it. I decided that something along the same lines would be just as popular, so I showed *House of Flying Daggers,* another beautifully made Chinese epic, which I had to reassure them was not actually about a house filled with flying daggers.

As soon as the movie began, Hazel yelled as loud as she could from the darkness, "What is this crap?"

Like lemmings off a cliff, the residents turned on me en masse.

"Turn it off."

"Where do you think we are, a fringe festival?"

"Booooo."

"What the hell is going on here?"

"I'm not paying for this."

And on and on the heckles came.

The next activity was the Men's Club. Our men's club was doomed from the first time I put it on the activities calendar. The men in our community, perhaps about ten percent of the total, rarely came out for any event I organized. With the usual exception of Ariel, who came on every bus excursion out for lunch (where he would then always complain that the meals in restaurants these days were too large for any respectable person in their right mind), and Tom, who religiously attended Fun with the Internet, where he would always insist on being shown "this internet porn that I keep hearing so much about."

I had three diehard fans of the Men's Club—one of which would always excuse himself early in the hour to go have diarrhea, another who would excuse himself repeatedly throughout to go have diarrhea, and the third who always assured me he would never come again because sitting in his room alone was so much more enthralling. However, not attending would deprive him of a forum in which to complain. So, he always showed up.

It was early in the day, so all four of us were still in attendance.

"I hope you don't expect us to play any games. Last week you went and turned this meeting into a carnival," said Arnold.

"You can't expect us to just sit here," Ken said.

"I don't know what's wrong with the staff here," said Sol. "When I moved in, I gave specific instructions that I didn't want to see my wife, and twice she's been escorted to my room. What don't they understand about my very simple request? I've had to be hospitalized because of her. Don't they understand that? It's not a joking matter. I'm still not well, and last night this caregiver shows up at my door with my wife. What the heck is wrong with these people?"

Sol and Henrietta had been married for forty-seven years. She had been difficult to live with before her Alzheimer's, he claimed. Her Alzheimer's made her intolerable. Sol and their two daughters had each been on anxiety medication for years; they jumped each time their cell phones rang. Henrietta called them each dozens of times every hour, checking to see where they were, what they were doing, and who they were with. Her insecurities would bubble up, then explode from her mouth with accusations and hurtful insults.

Sol had broken down and was hospitalized, hoping for death in order to be free of her. Their daughters had been close to their own mental and emotional breakdowns when their mother's intolerable personality, increasing dementia, need for constant supervision, feeding and care finally forced them to seek out a secure environment for her, far away from all of them. Henrietta and Sol moved into our community simultaneously, though Henrietta was moved into the Family Circle and Sol into our assisted living, with explicit instructions that his wife's constant demands to be taken to her husband should never be granted. On both occasions that her request was granted, the staff members had come from countries of origin that did not accept the separation of a husband and wife.

I looked up from behind the television where I was attempting to plug in my digital camera. "No games. No talking. No fun. Don't worry, you're safe here," I assured Arnold. Our men's club was its usual painful ordeal. I finally found the correct attachment and pushed the TV back into place. A grainy image had come up on the screen.

"What are we looking at?" Sol asked.

"What does it look like?"

"The Gulf of Mexico?"

I traced a curving line with my finger. "This bit here. It's not the edge of a meteor crater. See this. Where have you seen this shape before?" I turned to the side, displaying my profile.

"It looks like an x-ray," said Arnold.

"That's not a bad guess," I said.

"What's it an x-ray of?"

"It's an ultrasound inside of Angie's belly. You're looking at my child."

"What's wrong with it?"

"Nothing's wrong with it. At least, I hope nothing is."

The truth is that I had been worried about the integrity of my sperm since the time I had had an x-ray as a child, and the technician had forgotten to put the lead blanket over my midsection.

"Little Kevin's going to be a daddy," said Ariel from the doorway of the room. He started walking toward us. They were all excited and shook my hand.

"Fatherhood is the greatest gift you'll ever receive," Arnold said.

"I'm pretty scared."

"There's nothing to be afraid of."

"Sure, there is," Ariel said. "Pray your kid's not a prick."

"I have two daughters," Sol said, "and they're wonderful. Even at their worst, I love them dearly. No matter who your kid turns out to be, you're going to love them like they're a saint. My wife, on the other hand, I can't stand. But you'll see that there's no love like that you have for your child. It's unconditional."

For the rest of the morning, my spirits were lifted in a way I hadn't felt in a long time. I wasn't as afraid about the prospect of becoming a father. It helped to talk with those who had already been there and made the mistakes that I was so worried about making, and then realizing that things turned out just fine anyway.

Then I thought of Selma and her black eye and how her son Anthony had accused me of striking her. I had avoided Selma all morning. I was afraid to hear that that was what she believed had happened. There would be no recovering from an accusation like that. I would lose my job, my credibility, and the respect that I had gained. What I was most afraid of was not necessarily the accusation itself, but how quickly my life could be thrown into chaos and uncertainty. No matter how far we come along any path, no matter how well laid we think that path might be, and how difficult it had been for us to lay the groundwork in the first place, it could be torn up from under our feet with virtually no effort at all. And once that happened, we can never again get back to the same place, regardless of what we say or do.

After lunch, I sat with the Three Musketeers, Iris, Marcia, and Betsie, at a table next to the coffee bistro, sipping our hot beverages. We had begun our afternoon with a short game of Go Fish but had now moved onto the more important pastime of making a castle by stacking the cards together. Betsie's tremor kept knocking the stack down, but the other two ladies were good natured about this, and kept encouraging her to continue. The phone at the front desk began to ring. I looked up and saw that, as usual, Jennifer was nowhere in sight. I walked over and answered it. "Gleeful Meadows, this is Kevin."

"Hello, my name is Betty Tucker, and I'm coming to visit my Aunt Iris."

"What a coincidence, I just happen to be playing cards with her," I said.

"Oh great, I just wanted to call ahead to make sure she's finished lunch already. I'm taking her out for ice cream. Please let her know that I'll be there in about five minutes."

After I hung up, I walked back over to the table. The cards were in a sad little pile on the floor. Iris and Marcia were complaining about not having been served lunch, and Betsie was stuffing tissue and Post-it notes into her purse. "Finished with the cards already?" I asked.

"We got bored," Marcia said.

"Guess what, Iris?" I said.

"You're going to help spring us from this place?"

"Ha ha, very funny. No, your niece is coming to take you out for ice cream."

"Well, that's almost as good, I suppose."

"You sure are hard to please."

"I want ice cream too," Marcia said.

"I'll see if I can sneak some out of the kitchen for you. Is that good enough?" I asked.

"Alright."

I turned to the front entrance as a woman came through the door holding a baby in her arm. She walked straight over to our table, put her little girl down on the floor, and began to hug the Musketeers.

"It's so good to see you guys," she said. "It feels like it's been forever."

The ladies reciprocated with hugs and kisses. Marcia turned her wheelchair to get a better look at the woman. Betsie didn't look up from her purse.

"It's good to see you too," Iris said before getting a nice big kiss on the cheek.

The woman then looked down to the floor and saw that her little girl had crawled away. She ran over to the corner of the room and picked her up.

"Who is that woman?" Iris asked.

"That's your niece," I said.

"My niece? I don't remember ever seeing her before."

"Her name is Betty."

"I think that name's familiar, but I don't remember no baby."

The woman came back over to us. "I'm just going to go say hi to some of the other ladies. I'll be back in a bit."

"I guess she's made friends during her visits here," I said as I shrugged my shoulders.

"My niece? I don't think so," Iris said.

I put my hand on hers. "She wants to be close to you. She wants her daughter to know you."

Iris sighed. "Alright. I'll go get my jacket." She got up and left for her room.

I turned to the other two ladies. "Another game of Go Fish?"

"Excuse me," a voice said from behind me. I turned to see a woman in her sixties, who bore an uncanny resemblance to Iris. "I'm here to pick up Iris."

"You are?"

"Her niece, Betty. I called a short time ago."

I stared at her for a moment, confused. "Room 408," I said finally. "She went to get a jacket."

A few minutes later, I tracked down the first lady with the baby, who was now chatting with a couple of the cleaning staff. "Excuse me. Who are you?"

"I'm Karen. I used to work here."

Crap, I thought.

"Why, what's it to you?" she asked abruptly.

"Nothing. Just really amazingly strange timing."

"What's his problem?" I heard her ask as I walked away from them.

Nothing like confusing the already confused. Oh well, knowing Iris, by the time she put on her jacket, she wouldn't even remember that it wasn't the same woman who had come to collect her.

I decided that it was finally time to talk to Selma. I asked two care staff to go into her room with me so that there would be witnesses to the conversation. I felt dirty. I had spent so much time in our resident's rooms, chit-chatting and gossiping, just them and me, and I wondered now if that was all something of the past.

Selma came to her door and let us in. Her face looked awful. A deep purple stain stretched from beneath her left eye. "Hi, Selma, may we come in?" I asked.

"Of course." She moved aside and then closed the door after us. "What can I help you with?" Selma asked. "This looks so official."

"We wanted to ask you about the bruise on your face," I said.

She touched her cheek. "I must look terrible."

"You've looked better," I said with a smile.

"Did I ever tell you about the time I got a bump on the noggin' from sailing? Anthony had taken me sailing for the day. Not in a big sailing ship, you understand, but more of a dingy with a mast and sail. Anyway, I stood to get a better view of a school of fish that was swimming not far from us. Just then, a wave caused the boat to pitch, and I went into the sea. When I came up—I had on a life vest, of course—I smacked my head on the side of the boat. I was too heavy for Anthony to pull back up over the side, so he had to drag me back to shore before they could pull me from the water."

"How did you get this bruise? The one you've got now," the caregiver asked abruptly.

"Who knows? I must have whacked myself on my nightstand during my sleep."

"Is that what you told Anthony?" I asked.

"Pretty much. Why?"

"Sarah, our nurse," the caregiver cut in, "the one who examined you this morning? She said that you told Anthony that Kevin gave you that black eye. That he had struck you."

"What? Anthony told her that?"

I nodded.

"He must have been joking. Why would he say that? I never said anything like that. I love you. I can't believe he would tell her that."

"I need you to talk to Anthony," I said. "Sarah is going to submit an incident report to the state authorities, and once she does that, it cannot be rescinded."

Selma grabbed me, wrapping her arms tightly around me. She sobbed uncontrollably. "I'm so sorry. I don't want you to get in trouble. I'll wring that boy's neck. I don't know what's gotten into him to say something like that."

An hour later, I waited outside Paul's office while he and Anthony had a meeting. Finally, Anthony opened the door and left, shaking his head. He walked over to me. Anger was evident in his expression. He reached out a hand to me, and I shook it. "You want to tell me what kind of a world we live in where people take everything so damn seriously. I said it as a joke. I even had a smirk on my face as I had said it. I never imagined that that dimwit would have taken it seriously."

"Don't be mad at Sarah," I said. "She was just looking out for your mom."

"This damn world."

The slideshow of residents that I had begun a few months earlier had become a fun little side project that I worked on in my spare time. I had narrated it and filled it with images of our residents participating in activities. When it had been completed, I showed it to Paul. Paul was so impressed that he, in turn, showed it to his boss at the head office, who, in turn, had showed it to the owner of the company. They had listened to my idea of using it as a marketing tool, as opposed to the brochures currently being used, that featured geriatric models. They had their marketing firm design a DVD case for the slideshow and had given me complete control over the DVD itself and the screen printing of its face.

It had been a much larger project than I had anticipated but had had a much greater outcome than I could have anticipated as well. I had to get written approval from all residents in the slideshow or from their powers of attorney. After several weeks of phone tag, faxes, mailings, and chasing down people in the hallways, I had received all the signatures I needed. There were a few holdouts, but I just edited them out of the slideshow with Photoshop, cutting their heads from their bodies and transplanting the heads of others.

What a concept, a large corporation using real people in their marketing campaign. The significance to me in this particular situation was that this was somehow a victory for the senior population over ageism.

After work, I drove to pick up the DVDs from the printer. They looked wonderful. As I drove home, I was filled with such a sense of pride and accomplishment. At a red light, I picked the top disk off of the pile and looked at it. Screen printed on each DVD was the photograph I had taken of Tom kissing Elsie on the cheek. Such a positive symbol for our aging community. Below that it read: *Gleeful Meadows Assisted Living. Your personal tour of our comunity.*

Something didn't seem quite right. I read it again. Doesn't the word community have two Ms? I wasn't sure. I ran the word over in my head. I was a terrible speller, but that was what spell-checking programs were for. Surely, I was wrong. Wasn't I? Could they have made a mistake at the printers? Surely not. As I considered both spellings of the word, the debate was settled as I drove past the Jehovah's Witness Congregation and *Community* Center.

Crap!

Unbelievable. The Jehovah's Witnesses didn't even have to show up at my doorstep during breakfast to put me into a foul mood. I turned my car around and drove back.

I dropped the box of 1000 DVDs onto the counter back at the printers. "You guys spelled community wrong."

The clerk picked the top one off of the pile and looked at it for much longer than necessary. He put it down and looked at the next one, as though it could possibly be different. "Whoa, that sucks," he finally said after putting the disks back in the box.

"Uh, yeah," I said. "That sucks. How long is it going to take you guys to fix it?"

"Well, it's not really our problem, I'm sorry to say."

"What do you mean it's not your problem?"

"We sent you the proof before we started the screen printing. You signed it and sent it back." He pulled out a file and showed me the proof with my signature on it. "You okayed the disk label." He fingered the word *comunity* on the proof. "Sorry, bro."

"Don't bro me. I thought that the proof was to make sure you guys got the picture right. I didn't know I was supposed to check your freakin' spelling too. I'm not an English tutor."

"Excuse me, I've got other customers."

"I'd like to speak to your manager."

When the manager came over, I explained my predicament, how I was a lowly peon working on a special task for the brass of the company, and that I could neither deliver the disks in their current state to my boss, nor could I afford to pay for them to be reprinted. If I put another charge on the company credit card, they'd want to know why the price was not what I had told them it would be.

He was reasonable, and clearly took pity on crying, hysterical adult men. He suggested a compromise to meet me halfway: the order would be reprocessed, I would pay for the disks, and he would cover the cost of the labor. Since I had no other option, I agreed, handing over my own personal credit card to keep this situation from tarnishing my image of competence at work. I wondered about my image of competence at home when Angie finally saw the credit card statement.

When Angie got home that night, I was again in front of the computer. Paul and the company brass were expecting the disks the next day, and the soonest the new order could be ready would be a week.

"What are you up to?" Angie asked.

"I'll tell you the whole story on the drive out to work."

"Tonight? It's nearly eleven."

"I messed up and am trying to fix it."

She picked up one of the disks from the box next to me. "Hey, these look great." There was a pause. "Did you know that community is spelled wrong?"

As I drove, I told her the story of what had happened. I had bought a large box of adhesive labels the exact shape and size of the DVDs and spent the night reproducing the disk image on my own computer. When Angie and I arrived at Gleeful Meadows, we spent the next several hours covering up the silk-screened image with the ones I had printed at home on my laser printer. They didn't look as fancy as the silk-screened ones, but at least they were spelled correctly.

I had Angie check the spelling just to be sure and then left the entire box on the floor in front of Paul's office.

CHAPTER SIX

Interlopers

The next day, Paul didn't have time to notice the DVDs I had left for him the previous night. He had another problem on his hands. Lily L, who had moved in two weeks earlier, had fallen asleep in a lawn chair out in the sun and burned her face. Lily's daughter was livid. Unfortunately, this was not the first time in Lily's short tenure at Gleeful Meadows that she had fallen through the care cracks. Inexcusable once. Unthinkable twice.

The day after she had moved in, the weekend shift, which, for whatever reason, had not been informed that we had acquired a new resident, left Lily in her room all weekend. On Monday, she was found lying in her soiled bed, hungry and afraid. This was a case of miscommunication so extraordinary that you would have thought, from then on, Lily would be treated as though she were royalty.

Lily spent most of her time in bed on most days anyway. She was a holocaust survivor who, as far as we all knew, had had the spark of life within her extinguished long ago by experiences that the rest of us could scarcely imagine. She had been the only surviving member of her entire extended family. She didn't speak, never looked any of us in the eyes, and had no visible emotions. As Ariel so tenderly put it, "She's dead inside, her body just doesn't know it yet."

Her daughter, Maggie, on the other hand felt quite the opposite.

"Well, how long was she outside for?" Maggie asked.

"Not more than an hour," Paul said.

"An hour? Look at her. She looks like a sun-dried tomato."

Lily sat on a sofa in the corner of the foyer like a wilted flower. Her face was slick from an application of aloe vera. "She's here so she can be taken care of, and yet, time and again, she's neglected."

"I'm sorry about what happened. She likes to sit out in the sun. We can't make her come inside if she doesn't want to."

"What am I paying you for if you're not going to look after her?"

Then Paul, sounding like a complete asshole, said, "If you'd like to discuss her care plan, I would be happy to discuss it with you in my office."

To which Maggie responded, "There's no need. I'm taking her out of here. The state ought to shut this place down."

I thought about everything Maggie had said and about everything I had seen since coming to work here. Most people were doing their best for the residents. But was their best good enough? Didn't these people deserve more than the best that some of us were capable of offering? Truthfully, I wouldn't have put my parent in Gleeful Meadows, because I had firsthand exposure to some of the goofs and gaffs behind the scenes, which have made me shake my head, laugh, and cry. However, perhaps this was the case with all facilities. Everything could run better in a perfect world, but the world we live in has far deeper flaws than we would ever want to acknowledge, and the people handling our money, treating our wounds, engaging in activities with our seniors, flipping our burgers, and tucking our mothers and fathers in at night are sometimes far less competent than we could ever imagine. When industries like assisted living refuse to pay more than bottom dollar for their care staff, they are often left with the gunk on the bottom rung of the employment ladder. The result is that the people we care for most in the world end up being looked after by some of those least qualified to do so.

Word had circulated around the community about Angie's pregnancy. I was planning the same unveiling of the ultrasound for the ladies that I had given to the gents the previous day, but it seemed that no one is ever too old, too sick, or too stricken with diarrhea to listen to, and then pass along, a good piece of gossip.

"You're married?"

"How many kids do you have?"

"Who's Angie? Does she work here?"

"Who would marry you?"

"Look at the size of your own belly; you're sure you're not the pregnant one?"

"I hope the baby's born at least nine months after your wedding night."

"Is it a boy or a girl?"

"Kevin's got a baby?"

"How old is it?"

"When can we meet the little one?"

"What little one?"

"When was he born?"

"When was who born?"

"What is everyone talking about?"

"That reminds me of when they gave me the wrong baby at the hospital."

The accordionist, who had just spent the past hour enthralling our residents with his musical savvy, stopped me at the front door after his performance so I could cut him his check. "Would you like to schedule something now, or shall we connect over the phone?" he asked.

"I'll call you." The gentle way of saying that I never wanted to hear or see him again.

Ariel came by, dragging his walker behind him. "Thank you so much for coming to play for us," he stuck out his hand to the accordionist. "You're very talented."

The accordionist took his hand. "Thank you."

Ariel went on, "It was extremely monotonous, but that's not your fault. It's just the nature of your instrument."

During lunch, Selma held her mouth open as Sarah peered into the open orifice with her penlight. Sarah pulled away. "All present and accounted for," she said as she turned to the bowl of soup on the table in front of them, which had a rotten, fleshy tooth floating atop the creamy surface. It looked like a discolored piece of corn that had been twisted from a decaying husk. But, of course, it wasn't. It was, without a doubt, a tooth.

"Then whose tooth is it?" Selma asked.

"Perhaps it's just chicken gristle. You know, our chef makes his soups from scratch."

"Don't try to lay one over on me. I was gutting chickens before your parents were born. I want to see the boss."

What was still in question was whether the tooth was human or animal. If it was human, then wasn't someone missing it? If it was animal, then one wondered about the quality of production the food went through. Did they just push the entire animal, from nose to tail, into some gigantic blender and hope for the best?

Sarah remembered the sandwich with a hair in it from the previous week that Selma had kept in a plastic bag for four days before she finally had had her audience with Paul. She reached for the bowl.

"Don't touch that. That's my evidence," Selma said.

"Evidence of what?" a voice asked from somewhere else in the room.

Sarah knew that she had to quash the situation quickly and definitively before it spiraled either upward or downward in a cacophony of agreement and/or disagreement amongst the masses. A distraction was called for. Distractions were definitely found in abundance at Gleeful

Meadows. "Marge, I hear that your father was a governor," Sarah said to a hunched, diabetic woman with one missing leg.

"What's that, dear?" Marge asked.

"What about my soup?" Selma said.

"What's wrong with the soup?" someone asked.

"Who's soup?" someone else asked.

Sarah raised her voice. "I hear your father was a governor."

Marge nodded.

"I want to see the boss," Selma demanded.

Marge stared at the table contemplatively, and then began to tell her story on autopilot. "To put it kindly, my father was 'difficult.' To put it more accurately, he was an asshole."

"Who's an asshole?"

"Whose asshole?"

Mission accomplished.

"He was never very loving to those close to him." Marge paused for a moment before resuming. "And because heartfelt conversations were not encouraged between the generations in our family, we didn't know whether his emotional distance was due to his lack of desire, or simply a lack of ability due to some character flaw.

"He suffered a stroke about a year before his death, which, not surprisingly, made his winning personality more caustic. While researching the various care facilities for us to place him in, I was filled with an ever-present sense of foreboding concerning his ability to get along with the other patients housed there—or their ability to get along with him, whichever the case may be. Over his life, he has been ejected from sporting events, movie theaters, amusement parks, clubs (the Elks kind, as opposed to the dance variety), and once, most shamefully, from my younger brother's own eleventh birthday party. However, that is a story for another time and forum."

It was at that point in Marge's story that I came into the dining room with Nellie B and her daughter, Tess.

"Hi, everyone, I'd like you all to meet our newest resident, Nellie." There was an eruption of sparse claps.

Marge didn't hear the distraction because both her hearing aids sat on the table next to her, and she continued her story, even though no one was now listening.

"I can't stay here. These people are old," Nellie said.

"Mom, most of them are the same age as you."

"But they're old in spirit. I can tell just by looking at them. You know I only date men in their sixties."

"Yes, and that's a source of continual embarrassment for me. As I'm sure this moment will be as well."

"I can't help it if your friends find me more interesting than they find you."

"Don't be rude to these people. Please."

"As soon as you leave, I'm packing my things and getting a taxi."

"Where will you go? You've sold your apartment," Tess said.

"I'll live on the street."

"I would love to see that."

"Somebody," Nellie said to nobody in particular. "I need pain medication. I'm in so much pain."

"Grow up, Mom." Tess turned to look at Sarah and me. "She's such a faker."

"Is there a cat around?" Nellie asked. "My eyes are watering."

Paul's voice came over our walkie-talkies, "All senior staff please come to my office."

I left the dining room as Nellie went into a very well-acted, or psychosomatic, coughing fit. It was later confirmed by her daughter, who had four cats, that her mother had no such allergy.

Paul sat on the edge of his desk and began as the last of us filed in. "Some of you may have heard about the apartment fire not far from here that took place over the night."

"I heard two people were killed," Greg, our maintenance director, said.

"It's gone up to four. Anyway, it was an independent living senior's home, and we, along with several other senior's homes have agreed to help out by taking in one of their residents."

"Wasn't that place Section 8 housing?" Shana asked.

"Section 8?" I asked.

"Subsidized low income," Greg said.

"That'll go over well with our residents, who each spend a fortune to live here."

"This sounds like a PR gimmick," Eva said.

"It is what it is," Paul said. "Our new resident will be arriving this evening and will be staying with us for an indefinite amount of time free of charge. All courtesies will be extended to him."

Later that day, I stood just inside the front door of the reception area. The taxi driver and the passenger next to him sat talking for several minutes. I couldn't see the passenger's face, though his silhouette was reminiscent of Albert Einstein. Finally, he got out, and I went out to greet him. Clifford R had the tan of someone who spent most of their time asleep beneath the noon sun. He had shaggy, unkempt gray hair, and wore shorts that were too short, flip-flops, and an unbuttoned Hawaiian shirt. In each hand, he held a black garbage bag.

"So, you drew the short straw?" he said upon my approach.

"Pardon?"

"To be my welcoming committee."

"Oh, I guess so."

"No red carpet?"

"It's at the cleaners. Someone puked on it. Can I help you with your...luggage?"

"The rest's in the trunk."

As if on cue, the driver popped it open. I went around to the back of the cab and looked down at the single, large cardboard box. I lifted the lid and peeked inside. Beer and whiskey stared back at me.

"Hungry?" I asked.

"Famished."

There were still some stragglers in the dining room when Clifford and I entered. They smiled at me, and then frowned at Clifford. We walked to a table where Grace and Tom were sipping coffee. "Hi, guys. This is Clifford," I said.

"Cliff," he corrected. "How do you do?"

"We take people off the street now?"

"Grace, am I going to have to string you upside-down from the flagpole again?" I asked.

Tom stuck out his hand. "Name's Tom. Good to meet ya."

"Grace is our resident council president," I said.

"Don't tell anybody," she said. "I might actually have to do some work."

Cliff reached into his cardboard box and pulled out a bottle of Jack Daniels. "I'm having a housewarming party later on, if the two of you would care to join me."

"A man after my own heart attack," Grace said.

Bingo was a curse I had to endure three times a week without reprieve. Every other activity was relatively fluid and could be moved around or tossed off the calendar completely at a whim, without anyone caring or even noticing. Bingo was another story. It could not start late. It could not be postponed or altered in any way. The ladies were fanatical about it. They would arrive early, pick their lucky chairs, stack their chips just right, pick cards with certain numbers in certain positions, and then stare at me as I set up, as if watching for some kind of sleight-of-hand trickery.

Initially, we used the traditional rolling bingo basket with balls, but since no one had eyesight keen enough to see the balls (Adeline, on several occasions, accused me of intentionally calling out the incorrect number to either sabotage her or to help someone else), and those with hearing aids complained when I used the microphone, the traditional set had then been replaced by giant flash cards that I would shuffle in between each game.

Even though I was the one who bought the prizes, I considered them pretty lame. They were the best I could afford on my monthly activity budget—candy bars, soda, and whatever else I could find in the discount bin at Target. Though it wasn't the prizes that drew them. It was apparently the excitement. Excitement that did not filter up to me as I stood at the front of the room and endured for a complete thirty-six hundred seconds. I always began to sweat profusely, embarrassed by the same jokes I dished out each passing week.

Fortunately, on this particular day, I was saved from the remainder of bingo by Elsie who, without warning, went limp and collapsed in her chair. At one hundred and two, this is an alarming sight indeed, so I rushed over, as those around her yelled for help. She was still breathing, and, after a moment, came to. Fortunately (for me and Elsie), one of our nurses had been in the room at the time, perhaps enraptured by the excitement of the game.

Elsie was groggy and looked around at us. "I'm so tired," she said. "Did I fall asleep?"

"I thought you died right next to me," Cora said.

Elsie smiled weakly. "I'm not ready to go just yet. Though I could use a nap."

The nurse helped Elsie into her wheelchair and escorted her back to her room. I wondered about Elsie's will to hang onto life so relentlessly. She had outlived all her friends, all her children, and even most of her children's children. Perhaps, no matter how long you live, life always seems short when you're looking at it from the back end.

After cleaning up all the bingo supplies (with the assistance of Bernice, whom I bribed with a Snickers bar), I walked out into the sunshine of our courtyard. It was a beautiful area, with lush flowers that often drew out deer from the nearby forest. Today, only Clifford, our newest resident, was out there, drinking a beer, with his face up to the sun.

I sat in the patio chair next to him. Without turning to me, he reached into the cooler between us and withdrew a tallboy. He gestured it toward me.

"I wish I could," I said.

"Not while you're on duty, huh?"

"I've already gotten in trouble for that once before."

"That's too bad. It's a nice afternoon for a cold one."

"Something tells me every afternoon is perfect for a cold one."

He smiled. "So, what can I do for you?"

"I was wondering if you'd like to come inside and join us for some activities."

"Knitting and bingo with old ladies. I don't think so."

"What do you like to do?"

"You're looking at it. Besides, we're not each other's kind of people."

"Most of them aren't like Grace. They're good people. Nice. My friends."

"Just the same, I'm pretty happy right here." He took a long sip and tilted his head back, looking up into the sun. He pulled his shades down from his forehead. "Yeah, this is nice."

"So, what are you going to do?"

"I told you, you're looking at it," he said.

"No, I mean, in the future."

"I know this hospitality is only temporary. Find another place I suppose." There was a strange clicking when he spoke.

"I read your profile."

"Checking up on me." The clicking was from his unanchored dentures, which shifted awkwardly every time he opened his mouth.

"It's my job."

"So, you're wondering what happened?" He scratched the fuzz on his chin.

"I'm just making conversation. You don't have to talk about anything you don't want to."

"Life isn't something that rolls out smoothly at your feet. It's more like a strobe light. It's got a rhythm that you can try to roll with, though sometimes it leaves you dizzy and afraid. Young wife and a distinguished university career. Flashes of a strobe."

Later, as I stood next to the front desk chatting with Jennifer, Ariel came up to us. "You should get a load of this receptionist they got where I get my teeth done. No wonder they charge an arm and a leg." Clearly not all seniors have had their sex drives curtailed by age and illness. The previous week Ariel had said to Nicole, our Family Circle activities director, that if it weren't for his catheter, he would give her the ride of her life.

"Hi, Ariel," we both said.

He pulled back his lips and exposed his gnarly, brown teeth. "Get a load of the after shot. They do great work there, don't they?"

I gagged at the sight of his teeth, which looked like two crooked rows of sunflower seeds. The fact that we're all granted a mulligan on our teeth when our baby set fall out, clearly did little in the way of persuading Ariel to take better care of those that came in after.

He wandered away saying, "Roses are reddish, violets are bluish, if it wasn't for Christmas, we'd all be Jewish."

I sipped my coffee.

A moment later, Nellie was pushed up to us in a wheelchair by one of our caregivers. "This is Nellie," the caregiver announced.

"Hi, Nellie," I said. "Nice to see you again. What's with the wheelchair?"

"I need to talk to someone about getting some pain medication. Everything hurts so much. I can barely move now."

"I'll let Shana know that she needs to get in touch with you."

"Can't you help me?"

"I'm the activities director. I don't have access to medication."

"What if I gave you some money to go to the pharmacy for me?"

"I'll tell Shana to come see you as soon as she's free."

"No, you won't. You're just saying that to get me out of here."

"I promise you, Nellie, I'm not humoring you or patronizing you."

"Alright. I'll be waiting." She tilted her head back toward her caregiver. "Ouch, my neck. Take me to the dining room. I need another cookie."

Out of the corner of my eye, I could see the slow-moving top of Mildred S's wig through the window, making its way along the side of the building. She came into view as she reached the glass door. I turned, pretended not to notice her, and listened as she fumbled with the door. Mildred was my least favorite resident. She was rude and thoughtless and spoke down to nearly everyone she encountered. In appearance, she looked like Yoda, with a gray wig combed into a tight bun.

Several moments later, she sidled up next to me. "I need to see Paul," she said to no one in particular.

"Paul's in a meeting," Jennifer said.

"He's never available when there's something important to talk about."

"I'll tell him to come find you later."

"When it's convenient for him?"

"If you're busy at that time, the two of you can arrange another time to meet."

"I don't like the way this place is run," she said.

I wanted to say I agreed with her but was held back by my desire to keep my job and also by the notion that I hated Mildred. Most people believed she was mean because she was in pain from illness and frustrated by her shrinking independence, but I believed she was mean because she was a crummy person at heart.

She placed her walker against a wall, drew out her cane, which had been hanging on her walker's crossbar, and walked toward the front door. I moved to hold the door for her.

"My daughter's taking me to an appointment. Be sure they save my dinner."

When Mildred returned that evening, she had forgotten that she had left her walker in the reception hall and not her room, and immediately started screaming that her room had been burgled.

I spent several hours in my office that night, preparing crafts for the following week, and had lost track of time. I reached toward the phone in front of me and picked up the receiver to call Angie. There was no dial tone.

"Hello?" a woman's voice inquired.

"Hello?" I inquired back. *Crap*, I thought. It was merely a call that came in at the exact moment I picked up the receiver.

"I'm looking for Gleeful Meadows. Have I reached the right number?"

"Yes, ma'am. My name's Kevin, the activities director. How may I help you?"

I spent the next hour describing every detail of our community, right down to the color of the tablecloths. We got inquiry calls from people so particular they wanted to ensure that every minute detail matched up with their tastes before they would consider visiting for a tour. We also received calls from very lonely seniors who just wanted someone to talk to. It was impossible to tell the difference, and really, the difference was irrelevant.

I read her out the weekly menu, the activity calendar, the square footage of the rooms, the make and model of the toilets in the rooms, the number of residents we currently had, ratio of men to women, procedure for moving in, procedure for moving out, how medical supplies are ordered, how medical supplies were distributed, earthquake and other natural disaster preparedness for the community, temperature on the thermostats in the common areas, and so on.

I then took her details: age, medical needs, interests and hobbies, and so on.

Then finally it was over.

"What was your name again?" the woman asked.

"Kevin."

"Oh, that's an unusual name."

"I don't think so," I said, puzzled.

"Sure, it is. Not for men, but for a young lady like you, it's very unusual."

What the...?

"Alright, then, thank you for calling," I said. I crumpled up the piece of paper on which I had written her information and tossed it into the garbage bin underneath the desk. She was most likely another caller from the geriatric psychiatric ward. I wondered if Millicent had passed out our phone number.

On my way out of the building for the night, I saw Cliff on the patio with a beer in his hand. I walked over and sat next to him.

He reached into a cooler on the ground next to him and withdrew a beer. He handed it to me. I cracked it open and took a long pull.

"You live here too?" he asked.

"Seems that way sometimes."

"You sound about as thrilled about it as the rest of us."

"Most people aren't too thrilled about living in assisted living."

"Or working in it," Cliff said.

I chuckled.

"Couldn't some of these staffers at least humor us with a smile?" Cliff asked.

"I consider my smile part of my uniform. Comes off once I get home."

It was his turn to chuckle. "I'm sure you've used that line before."

We sat in silence for several minutes, drinking our beers and enjoying the chill of the night. I thought about how easy I found it to get on with most of the seniors in the community and how different it was from my personal life.

Three of my grandparents died long before I was born, and the fourth passed shortly thereafter. I had lots of great aunts and uncles, but there was always a formality that existed in my relationship with them, probably since most of them were just on loan to us while their real grandkids were elsewhere.

On my mother's side, two great uncles, who acted as surrogate grandparents for my brothers and me, were both named Max and were both childless. One was the brother of my mother's mother, and the other was the brother of my mother's father.

My mother's mother's brother Max had been a decorated bomber pilot during World War II, and variations on his war stories were all we ever talked about with him. Returning to civilian life, I suspect, had been a hard adjustment for a man whose four-engine Halifax 3 proudly toted the name "Piss on You" along its side.

My mother's father's brother Max was a gentle, if highly odd, soul whose most constant company were the birds that flew freely within his tiny apartment, pooping wherever they may. I remember once as a child watching him drive away from our home following a visit and seeing his birds flap around his head within the tiny confines of his car.

On my father's side, we developed a closeness with my great aunt Clare, who had seen me riding on a bus by myself as a child and came over to say hello. I didn't know who she was. It was after that that she reached out to me and my brothers and became the closest thing we had to a grandmother.

However, much as I loved the octogenarians in my family tree, visits with them when I was growing up were more a reluctant obligation than a joyful celebration of shared bloodline. One particular incident, that will follow me forever like a blemish of shame, was a promise I made to my mother's mother's brother Max.

Before I moved to Australia, during a visit of Angie's back to Canada, my Uncle Max called me and said he wanted to take Angie and me to lunch before she again returned for medical school back in Sydney. I never returned his call. Several months later, I saw Max at a family gathering, and he asked why I never got back to him regarding lunch. I told him I had forgotten, but that wasn't the truth. The truth was that I couldn't be bothered to call. I didn't think he really cared, though I saw now in his eyes that he did and was hurt. It was a gesture of embrace on his part to the woman who would one day be my wife, and it was met by me with a shrug of the shoulder.

I spent the next year watching his health decline, planning to take him for lunch with Angie as soon as she returned for her next summer break. He passed away shortly before she returned home, and I'll always feel that, not only had I deprived him of something special, but Angie and I as well.

"How's the baby bump coming along?" Cliff asked.

"Textbook," I said.

"Morning sickness?"

"Nope. Angie neither."

He smiled. "The ladies around here are as excited as expectant grandmothers."

"I've become close with them."

"So how are you going to break their hearts?"

"What do you mean?"

"They think you're going to bring the kid into work with you every day. That they'll take turns looking after the little one."

"Who said that?" I asked.

"That's what I hear."

"That's not practical or possible."

"I don't suppose it is."

"I'm thinking of becoming a stay-at-home dad."

"You can leave all this glamour?"

"It's just a thought."

"Stay-at-home dad? That's got a funny ring to it. Don't suppose it ever popped up on your aptitude test back in school."

"If I had followed the wisdom of that, I would have ended up as either an astronaut or a cowboy."

"Mine said the same thing. Seems we both followed suit in one way or another."

"I suppose so," I said.

"If I had it all to do over again, I think the only change I would make is that I would like to have been a father. I would have had lots of kids. First, I would have taken care of them, and then, maybe now, they'd be taking care of me. Just maybe." He was silent for a long moment. "You best be running on home to your pregnant wife."

I stood, shook Cliff's hand, and then walked to my car. I turned back and looked at him. He was crying. That was the image that would forever stay with me when I would think of Cliff. Not that of the carefree soul that he pretended to be, but of the lonely man whose life had somehow fallen so far off course.

That was the last time I ever saw him. The very next day, which I had off from work, we had a surprise audit from the state. Since it was against the law to house someone in assisted living without proper medical documentation, Paul decided that his act of good Samaritanism ended when the risk of financial penalty was put on the table. While the auditors were being ushered around the property, staff members helped Cliff pack his belongings back into the garbage bags he had arrived with. He was driven to a bus station, and I am told he said he would be forever grateful for the hospitality and the roof we put over his head.

That night Angie, her belly, and I took a shower. Not the sensual experience it once was, now with a lot less shimmy room. As we switched places, so one could lather their hair and the other could rinse, Angie lost her footing and slipped forward out of the tub.

To her, the fall happened over a span of hours, during which she was incapable of finding purchase, as her arms moved upward, first against the slippery wall, and then against the shower curtain, which came away in her grasp as she went down. For me, the experience happened so fast that I didn't have time to reach out to her, or even to react.

Angie's knees smacked the inside of the tub, her hands landed on the floor outside the tub, and her belly landed upon the tub's lip.

Frantically, I shut off the water and helped her up. She cupped her belly.

"The baby," I said.

"Your big huge bum," she said.

"What?"

"Your big bum pushed me out of the tub," she said.

"I didn't even touch you." I put a towel over her shoulders and helped her step from the tub.

"It was your bum. It's so big."

"We have to get you to the hospital."

"I'm fine."

"You don't know that. We have to be sure."

"I'm a doctor. I'm fine." She again put her hands to her belly. "Ouch."

"Let me take you to the hospital."

"I said I'm fine. You and your big bum."

CHAPTER SEVEN

The Gospel of Mildred

In the beginning, God created the heavens and the Earth.

Now the Earth was formless and empty, darkness was over the surface of the deep, and the Spirit of God was hovering over the waters.

And God said, "Let there be light," and there was light.

And Mildred saw that the light was good and said, "Are you trying to burn my retinas? What's the matter with you?" So, God separated the light from the darkness. "Dimmer. Dimmer still," Mildred whined.

God called the light "day" and the darkness Mildred called "night." "I was the one who called it night," God said to Mildred. Mildred rolled her eyes, "Look at you all high and mighty taking credit for everything."

And God said, "Let there be an expanse to separate me from Mildred."

And it was so.

God called the expanse "sky."

And God said, "Let the water under the sky be gathered to one place, and let dry ground appear." And it was so.

God called the dry ground "land," and the gathered waters he called "seas." And God saw that it was good.

"Stop patting yourself on the back and insisting that everything you do is so great," said Mildred.

"Would you please shut up?" said God.

"Don't tell me to shut up; you're not the boss of me."

"Well, actually..."

"And another thing," Mildred continued. "Would it kill you to give me something to eat? Talk about cutting corners to save a buck."

Then God said, "Let the land produce vegetation: seed-bearing plants and trees on the land that bear fruit with seed in it, according to their various kinds." And it was so. And God saw that it was good. But still Mildred complained: "This was too bitter and that was too sweet."

And God said, "Have you no shame? Have you no graciousness of spirit?"

"So suddenly you're not a glory hog? You're the one who made me this way."

"And I regret it more and more each day," said God.

"All this fanciness, and yet I don't feel safe. How about a little attention to security?"

God made two great lights—the greater light to govern the day and the lesser light to govern the night. He also made the stars.

God set them in the expanse of the sky to give light on the Earth. And God saw that it was good.

"You call this creation? I have a niece with a funny lung who creates more with her eyes closed."

And God said, "Let the water teem with living creatures, and let birds fly above the Earth across the expanse of the sky."

And God saw that it was good.

"I have a good mind to call PETA on you," said Mildred. "I don't much care for the way you've boxed up all these animals in your so-called sea and sky."

God blessed them and said, "Be fruitful and increase in number, and fill the water in the seas, and let the birds increase on the Earth."

And God said, "Let the land produce livestock and wild animals." And it was so. And the sounds of the animals drowned out that of Mildred's complaints.

And God saw that it was good. It was reeeeaaaaalllllllyyyyyy good.

Then God said, "Let us make man in our image, in our likeness, and let them rule..."

"I have something to say," interrupted Mildred. "I have something to say." God continued to speak, and Mildred continued unbidden, attempting to speak over God. By the time Mildred had finished what was essentially a rant regarding her difficulty sleeping over all the sounds and smells of the animals around her, there was a naked man and woman standing not far from her.

"Oh my," she said.

God blessed them and said, "Be fruitful and increase in number..."

"Alright, that's enough. When I saw the brochures for this place it seemed classy, but now it's turned into a bawdy house. Quite frankly, I don't much care for the management, and I feel that your sales pitch to me was a lie of biblical proportions."

There was no response.

"Hello?" Mildred said. "Is anybody there?"

Then Mildred beheld a sign from heaven. And that sign read, "Closed for the Day."

The heavens and the Earth were completed in all their vast array.

It was the seventh day, and this God decided would be a day free of Mildred, her complaints, and her backseat creation. This would be a day of rest.

Resident council began the same way it always did, with Adeline and Mildred arguing about who should call the meeting to order. As council president, Grace owned that responsibility. However, she had only attended one out of the last eight meetings and, once again, was not in attendance to swing the ceremonial gavel calling the proceedings to order.

Mildred handed out a three-page outline for the meeting, which drew an immediate protest from Adeline, who was quickly silenced by a unanimous vote from those in attendance (except for myself, who was there only to record attendance and take minutes) to shut the hell up.

"Kevin, tell her—" Adeline began.

"I'm not allowed to speak," I reminded her.

"Mildred shouldn't be allowed to influence people with her literature."

"Someone's got to take control of this driverless bus," Mildred said.

"We have to vote on it. Tell her."

"I'm not allowed to say anything. The last time I threw in my two cents, you were the one who started the motion to have my mouth taped over."

"Can I start a motion to have both Adeline's and Mildred's mouths taped over?" Cora asked.

Everyone stared at me hoping, praying, pleading that I would add something constructive.

"Robert's Rules of Order clearly states," Mildred began.

"Oh, would you shut up?" Adeline said.

The truth was that, with the exception of Adeline and Mildred, no one else cared much about resident council. Or, if they did, promptly forgot about it the moment the next activity began. They attended for something to do. While taking the minutes, I recorded everything said during the meeting. Though, when it came time to type them out and give each resident their copy, I would omit most of the dialogue, which usually descended into verbal diarrhea sometime after the twenty-minute mark.

"Someone stole my left shoe last night. I demand a search of everyone's room."

"The prawns at last week's dinner weren't plump enough."

"The shower curtains in my bathroom are on the wrong way."

"My banana at breakfast was bruised."

"Did anyone see American Idol last night?"

"The floors don't match the walls."

"Can the Family Circle folks be sent to another facility? They smell funny."

"We need new floor mats in our showers."

"The sidewalk in front of the building is uneven."

"My daughter and my retarded grandson are coming for a visit."

Beneath all the irrelevant and ridiculous requests, observations, and suggestions was the enduring need we all have to be heard and for our feelings to matter. Most of the residents had outlived their friends and rarely saw their families. They had limited mobility, diminished cognitive function, and lived with the ever-present reminder that death was standing in the corner of the room doing a crossword. Gleeful Meadows was now their whole world, and resident council was the only place where they could exert a modicum of control over their lives. This was the only place where their opinion came close to mattering to someone.

"Your opinion doesn't matter to anyone," Mildred said to one resident. "You haven't even been here for a week yet, so you have no business saying that everything is just wonderful. Because it isn't. This place cuts so many corners that I wonder how we're not all walking around in circles."

This drew a laugh from Nellie, who had been dozing in the corner. "Haha, circles," she said and then fell back asleep.

"The food is lousy," Mildred continued. "The quality of the linens is poor. The furniture is old and falling apart. The staff are poorly trained, and none of the doors have automatic openers. They made so many grand promises when my son-in-law toured this facility, and they haven't lived up to a single one. Once they get your money, they couldn't care less if you're happy."

"Well, I'm happy," Marcia said.

"I'm happy too," Cora said.

As much as Adeline wanted to contradict everything Mildred said, I knew she wasn't about to get on the happiness bandwagon.

"You all settle for much too little." Mildred was about to say something further when the cell phone in the basket of her walker began to ring. She answered it.

I looked around the room at the faces staring at me, expecting me to take control of the meeting. I hated even being there. It wasn't the complaints that I hated so much. It was that I agreed with most of them and wasn't in a position to say so. I knew that the company, or at least my boss, cut every financial corner possible. But wasn't that how businesses stayed in business? What did I know? Who was I to judge or comment?

I wondered about the fees that the residents paid into the community when they moved in, the "community investment deposit," which we told them went toward the "continual beautification of the property." This loose definition apparently seemed limited to duct tape and rubber cement. While, at the same time, the owner of the company had fourteen luxury cars, the most recent a Bentley, paid for by the residents in this room, who were being nickel and dimed with the notion that a piece of crap can be made to look like chocolate cake. Their families saw the chocolate cake when they toured, but now these residents were tasting the crap, and there was no one around to listen but me.

"One of these terrible doors, which they refuse to fix, just slammed against me," I heard Mildred say. I looked over to her. She was halfway through the door with the phone to her ear, and her walker knocked over before her.

I moved to help her. I pushed the door open and picked up her walker. All the while she kept chatting into the receiver. "I know, and I've mentioned it so many times. Not for my own safety, you understand, but for those who are less mobile. Of course, Sunny Horizons has automatic doors."

Sunny Horizons was our newest competitor that had just opened up a few blocks away. They had been actively recruiting our care staff, and now the buzz of the new facility was starting to make its way through the residents and their families. I was starting to hear the name crop up in conversations between less-savory staff and less-satisfied residents, and brochures started appearing everywhere. The financial backers behind Sunny Horizons had no previous knowledge of senior care and had gotten into the business because they saw it as a way to make a whole lot of money really quickly. Paul wasn't worried and referred to those who built Sunny Horizons as "dumb money." That didn't take away from the fact that, over the next month, twelve residents moved over to Sunny Horizons. They undercut our rent and care fees and paid for the moving costs of anyone who moved from Gleeful Meadows.

As Mildred left and the door closed behind her, I said, "Maybe you shouldn't be on the phone, pushing your walker, and opening a door at the same time."

I used to believe the myth of the cute and cuddly senior which has been perpetuated by our collective consciousness (since we had a collective consciousness), and by greeting card companies and the media (since their inceptions as well). The geriatric population spans the personality spectrum just like any other demographic. So-and-so was, indeed, an asshole, not merely cutesy-cranky. The dirty old man somehow became endearing. Our grandparents didn't screw. At the very most, they made love (on their wedding nights for the first time) for the sole purpose of procreation. There were no pretzel-shaped sex positions. There was no kink, because, as everyone knows, that greatest of generations was too busy with the fate of the world in their hands to waste precious time using said hands to tie, gag, or spank anyone anywhere other than on the field of battle. But isn't it said that the bedroom is just another field of battle?

The reality, however, is that everybody's parents and grandparents and great-grandparents were once precocious, horny teens and young adults, and, if they were fortunate enough, they carried that sexual spark with them well into their golden years, and into the walls of senior care facilities everywhere.

Generations never change.

Nellie continued to complain about her phantom pain throughout the week. She took to borrowing sanitary pads from other residents and stacked them strategically throughout her room so that, should she succumb to her pain and fall, she would have a soft place to land.

Shana gave her a once-over and then a twice-over, during which Nellie lowered herself to the floor and assumed the fetal position. On the phone with Nellie's daughter, Shana was reassured that this behavior was typical of Nellie's modus operandi and that her pain was truly nonexistent. An hour later, Nellie lost consciousness and was rushed to the hospital by ambulance.

As the ambulance drove away, I was sitting with a group of residents in the activity room preparing to rehearse a play. We had been rehearsing our play for over a month. Each rehearsal, we had to start from scratch, and I had a feeling the actual performance wouldn't be much different. There were eight of us in the performance, two of whom could not remember from one day to the next that they were in the cast for a play, one who was deaf and needed to be elbowed when it was time for her to speak her lines, one who was blind and couldn't read the script, one who had such stage fright that twice she fainted on her way to rehearsal, one who thought being an actor would help him pick up chicks, there was me, and then there was Mildred.

"Can't anybody take this seriously?" Mildred asked as we waited for a caregiver to wrangle up Cora and Iris.

"It's not meant to be serious," I said.

"Theater is always serious business."

"This is hardly theater. We're performing *Fibber McGee and Molly*."

"They can still have the courtesy to show up for rehearsal."

"We talked about this already, Mildred. Remember, it's not their fault?"

"Well, it's not my fault, either, so why should I be inconvenienced by them?"

"That's part of living in a community."

"Hi there," Cora said as she sat down next to me. "What's going on?"

"You're late," Mildred said.

Iris sat down next to Hazel on the sofa across from us. "Late for what?"

"Rehearsal," Mildred said.

"We're going to practice a play," I said as I handed Cora and Iris each a script with their lines highlighted in yellow.

"I've never done any acting before," Iris said.

"That doesn't matter. We're just trying to have fun."

"It should matter," said Mildred. "We don't want to make fools of ourselves."

"My daughter is coming to watch when we perform," Dorothea said. "My arthritis is hurting so bad; I don't know if I can go through with it."

Mildred rolled her eyes, while I wondered how great it would feel to push her off of the roof or down a flight of stairs.

"I'm so glad that I came up with the idea for putting together this theater group," Mildred said.

Would Mildred try to take the credit for her own tumble down the stairs? The truth was that she had not given me the idea to form the theater group. She did, however, suggest the material for us to perform (her suggestion being too highbrow for the rest of us chumps), so I decided between an episode of *Fibber McGee and Molly* or *Airwolf.*

My activity roster was, in part, designed to shake loose Mildred from attendance. She tended to sour the experience for everyone, whether it was by taking credit for something that rightly belonged with someone else or by criticizing the activity or those in attendance. And when she criticized, she always did it in such a way that the target individual was made to feel as if, to speak up for themselves, they were somehow being petty or a trouble seeker. At the last meeting of our poetry group, she had said to Leona P, "I thought your choice for your favorite poem was silly. But, then again, you didn't write it, did you?"

I knocked on Paul's door and then opened it. He was behind his desk on the phone. He waved me in. I handed him my notes taken during resident council. He looked over them silently and bit the tip of his pen while doing so. He took the pen from his mouth and began making notes along the edge of the paper. After he hung up the phone, he looked up and said, "Did you raise your voice to Lloyd P earlier today?"

"Yes, I did."

"Don't ever do that again."

"He kicked my cat."

"This is his home. You're an employee here. If he doesn't want you bringing your cat to work, that's his choice."

"What if he kicked a Black employee because he didn't want them around his home either?"

"Don't bring your cat to work again."

"The residents love Kaz."

"Clearly they don't."

"One person doesn't."

"That's enough." He handed my notes from the council meeting back to me. Most of the page had been crossed out with red ink.

"Not much left," I said.

"We don't have the budget for most of it."

There was a knock on the open door. Paul and I turned to see Mildred. She came into the room and set a sheet of paper on Paul's desk. "I took the liberty of recording today's meeting with my Dictaphone. I just finished typing out the transcript, which I'd like for you to distribute to all the residents by this evening."

"Isn't that redundant, since Kevin already does the same thing?" Paul said.

"Does he? It seems to me that his minutes are always abridged. I just wanted to make sure that nothing was left out."

At that, Mildred turned around and left. Paul picked up the sheet of paper and sighed. He punched a few buttons on the phone on his desk.

"Yes?" Eva said over the intercom.

"Can I see you in my office?"

A moment later, Eva came in and sat down next to me. Her face was red, and she no doubt assumed she was in trouble for something.

"We've got to move on some things pretty quickly. Otherwise, we might be expecting a visit from the ombudsman." Paul floated Mildred's document over to Eva. She caught it off the edge of the desk. "Pick something on the list of demands that you can take care of today."

"Today? I've got to be available for tours." This was a marketing director's excuse to get out of doing almost anything.

"There'll be time enough for you to get back to your online shoe shopping," Paul said. Eva's expression angered. "Save the defensiveness for when it's warranted."

She loudly exhaled then looked down at Mildred's notes.

"Pick either the bathmats or a phone call to our paver to have that section of the sidewalk fixed," Paul said.

"Oh hell, I pick the phone call," Eva said. She turned to me with her thumb and index finger on her forehead in the shape of an L. "Loooooser," she said.

"Alright, Kevin, you're the bathmat guy."

"Bathmats for the whole community? I don't have time to go shopping. I've got activities to run all afternoon."

"Cancel one."

"And have another visit from the ombudsman because I'm not sticking to schedule?"

"You'll figure something out."

"Crap."

"Remember, cheap is the key word here," Paul said.

"How could I forget? I'm reminded every two weeks when I get my paycheck."

As Eva and I stood to leave, Paul's intercom buzzed. Jennifer's voice came through. "I've got Mildred on the line saying that she's got a physical therapy appointment in twenty minutes and is wondering where Kevin is with the bus."

I leaned forward. "Tell her she needs to give at least twenty-four hours' notice to book the bus for an appointment. Since she's such a stickler for rules, remind her that it's in the resident handbook."

"Damn," Paul said. "Mildred called yesterday to book the bus. Jennifer was away from the desk, so I took down the appointment. I forgot to tell you about it."

"So, what now? I can't spend the whole afternoon driving the bus for Mildred and then going bathmat shopping. I'll have to cancel more than just one activity."

"Cancel one to drive Mildred to her appointment. Then, when you come back, make the call to our pavement guy." He turned to Eva. "Looks like you're on bathmat duty."

I turned to her with an L on my forehead. "And when are you going to clear someone else for bus driver detail?" I said to Paul. "It's not right that I'm the only director who gets pulled away from my regular job with the residents whenever someone needs to be driven somewhere."

"I'm working on it. It takes time to clear the legal hurdles." This, of course, was bullshit. It had taken three days for me to be approved to drive the sixteen-passenger bus. Paul hadn't just put the paperwork on the backburner. It had fallen completely off the stove.

Nicole had been the other bus driver in the community. Unfortunately, a month earlier, she had reversed into a cement pylon at a gas station and knocked off the rear bumper. This minor fender bender had been witnessed by Paul, who happened to be at the station gassing up his car. This had been her second offense in the bus (well, second one that Paul knew about. I knew of three others that he did not). The first that had come to Paul's attention was when Nicole had swerved and sideswiped a city bus that had been driving next to her. In her defense, Nicole had been startled when the resident whom she had been transporting, one with severe Alzheimer's, had unbuckled his seatbelt, walked up behind her, and put his finger in her ear.

On my way out of the building, I walked past Eva's office and waved. She gave me the finger. Eva had been in a funk for most of the day, and now it was immeasurably worse as a result of getting the crummier of the two tasks to complete. She was having trouble with her boyfriend. She couldn't bring herself to break up with him, yet it made her sick to her stomach to even think of him. They hadn't spoken since the previous week when, in the throes of passion, he had accidentally blown a piece of snot out of his nose onto her. Having just come from an all-you-can-eat buffet, Eva was already a little queasy. The snot landing on her chest had pushed her over the edge, and she threw up all over herself.

As I walked to the bus, I passed Wesley Marie. I told her where I was going, and she asked if she could come. I told her no and that we would go for a walk later, and I would buy her a Popsicle at the store.

Her Alzheimer's had been advancing rapidly since she had arrived at our community, and now there was talk of moving her to the Family Circle. Other residents had begun to complain about her erratic behavior. Her diminishing social graces were a direct result of her disease, but most people saw only the symptoms, not the disease that caused them. I saw neither. I saw the residents treating my friend like a pariah, and the staff talking about locking her away behind the impenetrable gates of the Circle.

Wesley Marie had become so dear to me that I no longer thought about her continual care objectively. Instead, I thought about it in terms that were personal. I wouldn't see my friend as often if she moved to the Circle. She wouldn't have the freedom to carry out the routines that gave her life purpose. I was her only friend, so I thought, that truly had her best interests in mind. Or, more accurately, I had her best interests at heart. Because I was being swayed by my heart instead of my mind, I couldn't see what was so obvious to everyone else.

Wesley Marie had become a danger to herself.

She had begun waking up in the night and going out for long walks. This had been discovered by one of the night staff on a routine check of Wesley Marie's room. Before the staffer could call the police, Wesley Marie had returned, though her explanation of where she had gone was incomprehensible. When she snuck out the following night and returned covered in mud and twigs, with no discernible knowledge as to what had happened to her or where she had been, her fate had been sealed.

As I drove the bus slowly through the parking lot toward the front entrance where I would meet Mildred, I noticed Ken under the shade of a tree in his wheelchair, crying. Ken had just recently had his leg amputated due to a diabetic ulcer and had been trying to relearn how to walk with a prosthetic. He had joked with the ladies that he'd be back dancing in no time. The reality was that his hips had deteriorated so much in the six months that he had been off his feet that the pain he now felt while trying to stand was more than he could bear. Ken, who had taken a bayonet to the gut in Korea and had barely even noticed, now turned a sickly gray at the very thought of standing.

I picked up Mildred and drove her to her appointment. For twenty minutes, I listened to her complain about how, every day, her daughter tells her to move, but that she didn't feel her heart could bear another move. She told me about all the areas in which she believed we were in violation of one code or another, and areas where we dangled just within code, but could be in violation with just a sneeze or a strong wind. She told me again about the previous community she had lived in and that it was better in every way possible than ours. She complained about the beef being too tough, the vegetables not being fresh enough, and her neighbors smelling like bowel movement. I wondered if anyone would notice or care if the bus came back with only myself aboard.

Cooking with Kevin was more of a clumsy shtick centered around food than it was a cooking demonstration. After all, most of my audience were grandmothers who had spent years in the kitchen providing for husbands, children, children's children, in-laws, children's in-laws, and a host of other hungry mouths for the better part of a century. And the men in attendance, where their culinary skills were lacking, their taste buds had been refined and polished like delicate tools of deduction for having been cooked for during the better part of that same century.

No, my job here was to be a cooking buffoon, rather than a chef or instructor. The sillier, the better. The messier, the better. And whatever monstrous concoction I had attempted to produce on any given Wednesday was welcomed with applause and smiles and laughter, and then gratefully and graciously eaten. Whenever I would become confused by a recipe, my audience would shout out hints or suggestions, never letting me run too far astray from my intended destination. They were always the perfect audience when it came to interactive theater. That is, however, with the one exception of Mildred.

Mildred did not regularly attend Cooking with Kevin, as she could not understand why anyone who could cook better than someone else would want to sit for an hour and watch that someone else make a mess and a fool of themselves while producing sub-par cuisine.

On the day I made potato latkes for Chanukah, Mildred decided to grace us all with her presence. I had decided to make latkes because they seemed easy, and I wanted to share a little bit of my own culture with our residents, most of whom celebrated Christmas. Of the Hebraic persuasion at the community, there was only myself, Ariel, and Mildred. Oy.

I was flustered and embarrassed as I waited for the latkes to fry. I had spent the last twenty minutes under fire from Mildred, who criticized my every move in pursuit of fried potato perfection.

"Where did you get this horrible recipe?"

"Have you ever been in a kitchen before?"

"What's wrong with you? Tell me? Did your parents not hug you enough?"

"Who told you to rinse out the starch?"

"Flip them already. Flip them now, mister."

"Are you even really Jewish?"

"Our ancestors would vomit in their graves."

And on and on it went. I could see that the rest of the residents were as uncomfortable as I was, but they were as helpless as I at airing out the discomfort that now saturated the room.

Mildred handed her plate back to me with only a single bite taken from her latke. "It was terrible. Bland. No taste at all."

"Everyone else seems to like them," I said.

"They're just being kind."

"Well, perhaps you could learn a thing or two from them."

"I don't understand you. You had a perfect opportunity to share a part of our culture with these people, and you blew it."

"I didn't blow it, Mildred, you did."

"Oh, you're so full of yourself."

"Ask yourself which of us was truly a worse ambassador for our people here today."

"You were making a mockery—"

"We were having fun." Tears welled in my eyes. I wanted to shout at her that she was nothing but a bully. But bullies know we so rarely call them out for what they are. Our silence gives them the power, and so I silently stood, holding her plate as she walked away.

I had held a baby once previously in my lifetime. He smelled funny and spit up on me and seemed to push away from me the way two opposing magnets do. If I were being completely honest, it wasn't a great experience. There was nothing overly special or sweet about the experience, and I didn't feel an overwhelming urge to run right out and get one of my own.

Now, years later, in a prenatal class with Angie, it was time to hone those skills which had previously eluded me. I was given a ceramic replica of an infant and told to hold him (it was a him) for the remainder of the day as though he were a real baby.

"My arms are tired," I said.

"Switch positions," Angie said in return.

"I'm no good with my right hand."

"Don't put him down on the table."

"Wouldn't we have a crib or something?"

"Not if we were out."

"Then we'd have a stroller or a car seat. This exercise is completely unrealistic."

"You're being immature."

"I'm the one who's been holding it—"

"Him."

"I'm the one who's been holding him for the past three hours."

"You're doing great."

"I know, but now it's time for Mommy to do great."

"You're going to be at home with him alone for most of the day, so you're going to have to be comfortable with being uncomfortable."

We had decided that I would leave the workforce and become a stay-at-home father. It was a decision that we had not come to easily. Our decision was based partly on the cost of daycare, which was close to what I took home from work, and that neither of us (mostly me) wanted to have our child raised by strangers.

I'll be completely honest. The idea of never having to go to work again was really, really cool.

Though, the more I thought about what was in store for me, the less cool it seemed. There would be pee, poo, and puke on a constant basis. Surely nothing cool could ever be found in tandem with that dreaded excretory trilogy. It occurred to me that I didn't even have to venture any further into the alphabet for more cringe-worthy encounters that awaited me in daddyhood. Pampers, potty training, play dates, puberty, periods (if it was a girl), parole (if he was a delinquent). My goodness, what was I getting myself into?

Just then my cell phone rang. All the other expectant parents in the room who had had foresight enough to turn off their phones stared at me. I put the dummy baby on the table and flipped open my phone. "Hello?"

There were sobs on the other end of the line, then, "Kevin?"

"Yes?"

"It's Eva," the voice said through heaving breath and tears.

I excused myself from the room and went into the hallway. "What's wrong?"

"Ada slipped and broke her hip."

"Oh no. Is she okay?"

"They don't know yet."

I wondered why she had deemed it necessary to call me with this news. Falls and broken hips were common, even expected, in our industry. And why had the news been so devastating to her? Surely, she couldn't have been that close with Ada, or any of the residents for that matter. It was neither in her job description, nor her nature, to get very involved in the daily goings-on of the residents' lives.

"She slipped coming out of the shower," Eva said. "On the bathmat. The ones I bought."

Oh crap, I thought.

"They're going to blame me. They're going to say it's my fault," she said.

"No one is going to say that. It's not your fault. These things happen. They're just a part of life."

"It was the cheap bathmats. After they were washed and put in the dryer, the backing melted off of them. That's why it slipped." After a long bout of sobs, her voice came back on the line. It was faint and hard to distinguish, but the words were real and not my imagination. "It was supposed to be you who picked up those mats. Not me. This was supposed to be your fault," she said.

Curse Paul and his penny pinching. Then I thought about Mildred and the favor she had inadvertently done for me. If it weren't for her and her physical therapy appointment, I would have been the one who bought the cheap bathmats, and I would be the one who would now feel responsible for Ada's fall. In that moment, I hated Paul for insisting on the cheapest product, I hated Eva for her insistence that it should have been me instead of her who had bought the mats, and I hated Mildred for having saved me that task and the life-changing guilt that had snuck into the plastic shopping bag along with purchase and receipt.

Our company Christmas party was an offense to the sort-of-hard work that most of us did on a daily basis. Especially when compared to the soirées thrown for the staff at virtually every other organization throughout the country. Though even more so when viewed through one of the stained-glass windows of our owner's latest summer home.

Every aspect of the party was designed to save as much money as possible. Our party was held in the activity room at Gleeful Meadows so that no function hall needed to be rented. Unfortunately, this meant that no alcohol was permitted at the party. It was a potluck, with no dishes provided by the company. Meals were brought by staff, some of whom I wouldn't trust to do my laundry, let alone cook for me.

After we ate, we were presented with our Christmas bonuses, which came in the form of a tin of caramel popcorn for each person. Then, the evening was capped off with the scheduled entertainment—Paul had bought a roll of scratch lottery tickets, and we took turns scratching to see if that could possibly have been our last day of employment at Gleeful Meadows. All this merriment took place while we listened to classic carols on a portable radio, while the residents looked in at us through the windows with pity and wonderment.

I was the big winner of the night, with heartburn and a six-dollar winning scratch ticket. When I got home later that night, I thought about that man I had long ago met in Australia while we were both looking for work. I thought about him as I filled my mouth with caramel popcorn. Most staff were so offended by receiving only the popcorn for a Christmas bonus that they refused to accept it. Others emptied their tins on the driveway at Gleeful Meadows, or upon the lawn, or up into trees, which all had to be cleaned away by Greg and his assistant, Johnny, the next morning.

Partway through the task, Greg found footprints of white paint that led down one of the paths. He followed the footprints until he found Johnny with a can of white paint, painting, "Johnny was here," and "his place sucks," across the lawn.

"What the hell are you doing?" Greg asked him.

"Oh, hey, man," Johnny said to Greg. "Just letting off some steam. You know how it is. I'll get back to work in a minute."

Greg looked down at Johnny's shoes, which were covered in wet white paint. This incident with Johnny would grow to mythic proportions at Gleeful Meadows in the following weeks. Some people thought that he was protesting the plight of the underappreciated, underpaid worker, some people thought that he had gone nuts, and others figured he was just an asshole. Regardless of his motivation, jokes were made about the intelligence level of a man who could commit such intentional property vandalism at his place of employment and expect to continue working there.

"Get back to work?" Greg asked. "Dude, you're fired."

So, Greg not only had to finish cleaning up the littered caramel popcorn, but now also Johnny's mess as well.

I could understand the disappointment of those staff members, whoever they may have been, who littered the property with their Christmas bonus. Most of them were likely living paycheck to paycheck, for whatever reason, and were hoping for a little extra something to help them and their families through the holidays. On the other hand, Angie and I were comfortable. We didn't have much, but we lived frugally and were happy with what we had. But what set me apart from the disgruntlement of my coworkers was the thought of that unemployed man back in Australia, who would have given anything to have a job, let alone a Christmas bonus. He was just one man, but he represented millions of people all over the world in similar and worse situations than his own.

Angie wouldn't be home for hours to come. I laid back in bed while I drank a rum and coke and watched a movie. I shoveled caramel popcorn into my mouth as I gave thanks for my Christmas bonus. For reasons I was unsure of, I also thought back to when Mildred had stormed (as much as she was capable of storming) out of the kitchen after handing me the plate which held her partially eaten latke.

I was embarrassed by Mildred because I felt we were connected through our shared heritage. Her actions and words reflected on me and our people. I'm conflicted by my feeling toward her now, as I know she passed away shortly after I left Gleeful Meadows. I was ashamed, because I was relieved when I heard the news. What did this say about me? An old woman had died, and I was glad. A mean old woman, but someone's mother and grandmother. Surely, she also had friends somewhere, though I knew she had none at Gleeful Meadows. Someone must have been able to tolerate her, otherwise she wouldn't have had a family to mourn for her. Yet, to me, she was defined by my experiences of her. How could I see her otherwise? I wasn't obligated to like her for being elderly, sick, Jewish, or dead.

Then why do I feel guilty?

There was no memoir in the trash to tell me what Mildred had been like when she was younger. I knew she had been a mayor of a small town, but I knew little else. Had she become cruel and inconsiderate of others after her husband had died? When she herself became sick? Or had she been like that all along? Some are, and that's just a fact of life. The myth of the cute and cuddly senior was once again struck down before me.

CHAPTER EIGHT

Laughter and Tears

To: all_staff@gleefulmeadows.com
From: the_boss@gleefulmeadows.com
Subject: Watch your toes
Message: She's Baaaaaaaaaaaacccccccccccckkkkkkkkkkk!!!!!!!!!!!!!!!!!!!

It was a different Pennsylvania Dutch Millicent L who was wheeled into the lobby following her most recent stay at the geriatric psychiatric hospital. Her electric scooter was gone, and so, too, was the aura of menace that seemed to follow her wherever she went like it does with any other supervillain. The word on the street was that she had been medicated just enough to keep her from sliding out of her chair, but also enough so that she could no longer catapult herself onto the floor at will. The meds and lack of electric go-power promised to make a much more manageable Millicent. I suspect her newly adopted air of civility had come about in some small part from her knowledge that any further behavioral outbursts would doom her to live out the rest of her days in a geriatric psychiatric ward.

Millicent's hair was unkempt, and her makeup smudged and uneven. She sat askew in her chair, and her shirt buttons were not fastened properly. She looked like someone who knew she had escaped a horrible ordeal by nothing more than the skin of her false teeth. After the fanfare had died down, Millicent asked to be pushed to the reception desk where I was filling in for Jennifer while she was away on her lunch break.

"Kevin, may I make a phone call?" Millicent asked, her voice breathy, as though she had just run a great distance. Which, of course, was unlikely. "Pretty please." Her smile was weak.

"Of course." I picked up the receiver and handed it to her.

"Would you dial for me?"

"Any time you're ready," I said.

She read the number off of a slip of paper. After I dialed, she waited as it rang. "Hello, is this the Neptune Society...oh good...I'd like you to kill me."

I stared at Millicent with disbelief.

"...what do you mean that's not what you do...but I'm ready to go...I...I...was told that you...I want you to kill me."

I wasn't sure whether Millicent was making this call right in front of me for shock value, or if, in fact, she wanted to be put out of her misery.

"I haven't unpacked my bags yet. I'd like for it to happen as soon as possible, so I won't have to unpack them." She paused for some time. "Hello?" she said into the receiver. "Hello?" She looked up at me. "They hung up on me. How rude. Would you dial again for me?"

I took the receiver from her and hung up the phone.

"The Neptune Society performs cremations," I said.

"Yes, I know." She gestured to the phone again with her one good hand.

"People are supposed to be dead first."

"What's the difference?" she asked.

"Sort of a big one actually."

On my way to the activity room, I passed Tom B, who was seated in a lawn chair in the middle of the hallway with his head lowered. "Hey, Tom. What's going on?" I asked.

He looked up at me through tired eyes and, with a deep wheeze in his chest, said, "You're the guy that runs this here place, aren't you?"

"Not exactly. Are you feeling okay?"

"I was in too much of a hurry and lost my breath. Somebody brought me this chair to sit on a while back."

I knelt next to him. "Where were you going in such a hurry?"

Tom reached into his breast pocket and removed a crumpled piece of paper. He handed it to me. "I've got to get my whiskers chopped," he said.

I unfolded the piece of paper and read it. It was an appointment slip for the hair salon. "Your appointment is on Thursday," I said.

"What day's today?"

"Tuesday."

He squinted and chewed his lip as he thought. Sweat clung to the tip of his nose. He took a handkerchief from his breast pocket and wiped his brow. The drop on his nose fell onto his shirt, adding itself to a well-established wet spot. "I guess I didn't need to rush so much."

I put my hand on his wrist as I got to my feet. His arms were covered with bruises and tears from his aged, thinning skin. He had recently bumped into the edge of a dresser, which had torn a hole into his arm. "I'm going to go get one of the nurses to take a look at you," I said.

"Please don't. You get the officials involved and they'll call Mikey. That boy of mine is in worse shape than me. It gives him ulcers worrying about me. Please don't put his health in any more jeopardy than it already is. I don't know what I'd do without my boy. We're all each other have. I can hold my stuffing in for a little bit longer. Remember, I'm going to get my letter from the president."

"Tom, you're long overdue for your hundred-thousand-mile tire rotation."

"If I went running to the quacks each time I felt weak at the knees, they'd have me institutionalized."

"You are institutionalized," I said.

He smiled and let out a sound like an inner tube with a puncture. "Half the time I don't even actually fall asleep at night. Did you know that?"

I shook my head, not understanding.

"I faint and wake up on the floor." He chuckled as though he had heard a joke I had not. "Hasn't done me any harm yet. Besides, it's better than lying awake all night on my big comfy pillow and counting sheep."

After I deposited Tom and his chair at the nearest nursing station, I led the group in a combination of exercises and music appreciation. The booming voice coming out of the CD player was Luciano Pavarotti, or Lucky P, as perhaps he was known to his close friends. I led in some basic stretches, and then we finished by tossing a beach ball to one another. When someone caught the ball, they had to recount their fondest memory of childhood. Bernice had just told us of the time when she overheard her neighbor, Henry, telling his best friend that he was fond of Bernice. Henry and Bernice were married several years later.

Bernice had overheard the conversation on the phone, which, in that era, was not private, but instead on a single "party" line shared by several houses. In order to make a call, you had to first check that it was not already in use by, not only someone in your own home, but by one of your neighbors as well. This led to rampant eavesdropping on conversations. Children would snicker as they listened in, while covering the mouthpiece, and would later gossip about what they had overheard.

I was distracted from Bernice's reminiscing by the ringing of the activity room extension of the phone. Where the hell was Jennifer now? I wondered.

"Where the hell is Jennifer?" Hazel asked. "Would someone answer that damn phone."

I walked over and picked up the receiver. "Hello?"

"Could I speak with Cora?" said a young woman.

I looked over at Cora. "Who's calling?" I asked.

"This is Joan, her granddaughter."

I put the caller on hold and walked over to Cora, who was reading a newspaper in the corner of the activity room. "Do you know someone named Joan?"

"That's my granddaughter," she said without looking up.

"Would you like to speak to her? She's on the phone."

She sighed and flicked a piece of lint from the tip of a fingernail. "I'm not doing anything else." Cora folded her newspaper and then followed me over to the phone. I handed her the receiver and pushed the button to reopen the line. "Hello?" Cora said in a singsong tone.

I had broken one of the cardinal rules of senior care. I had allowed someone access to one of our residents without first consulting their guardian. As I watched Cora, my anxiety grew. I had no doubt that the woman on the other end of the line was who she claimed to be, but it bothered me that this was the first I had heard of her. I had become close with the residents, knew most of their close family personally, and at least the names of those whom I did not know personally. Cora didn't talk about her family, mostly because she could barely remember any of their names. But we had personal histories on file for all of our residents that we practically forced their families to complete. Why had I never heard or read anything about this prodigal granddaughter?

As the conversation progressed, Cora kept repeating, "Are you living in my house?"

I needed to know what the conversation was about, though I knew that Cora would forget by the time she hung up. Most likely, Cora couldn't remember what the conversation was about at *that* moment, let alone after it was completed. I surreptitiously tapped the volume button until I could just make out Joan's side of the conversation.

"I've just finished weeding the garden. I can't believe how overgrown it's become," Joan said.

"Are you living in my house?" Cora asked again.

135

"I've done a lot of work here. Not that the place'll ever be worth much."

"Who is this?" Cora asked.

"It's me, Joan."

"Oh, Joan. You're my granddaughter."

"That's right, Grandma."

"Have you finished school yet?"

"I finished school a long time ago. I'm not a little girl anymore."

"Did you finish school, or were just finished with it?" Cora laughed to herself.

"Grandma, about why I'm calling."

"You didn't just want to say hello?"

"We were talking about the house."

"My house? Are you living in my house?"

"It hasn't been your house for a long time now."

Cora looked across the room at some of the ladies playing cards. She was silent for a moment and looked as if she had forgotten she was even on the phone. She then looked at me and then again at the receiver in her hand. "Is this Joan?"

"Grandma, I wanted to know what you thought about me selling the house."

"My house?"

"It's not really your house anymore. Not really."

"Have you talked to your mom about this?"

"I'm talking to you. Would it be okay with you if I sold the house?"

Before Cora could answer, I reached over and pressed the hang-up button on the phone cradle.

Cora turned to me. "What did you do that for?"

"I can't very well have you occupy the phone here all day. What if I had an important call, like from a radio station or something?"

"You cheeky little fellow." She handed the receiver back to me, and then looked puzzled. "Who was on the phone?" she asked.

"Wrong number."

The first call I made when I got back to my office was to Cora's daughter. There was no answer, so I left her a message saying nothing more than that I had something I needed to talk to her about. My next call was to a senior's advocate who specialized in financial elder abuse. He told me not to call the family directly, that, as a possible witness to the alleged abuse, I needed to remain at an objective distance. I decided not to tell him that I had already put a call in to Cora's daughter. I described to him exactly what I had overheard (eavesdropped).

I had a sick feeling in my stomach, which did not improve later in the day when I received a phone call from Cora's daughter. "What did you want to talk to me about?" she asked.

I stuttered briefly while I searched my mind. "Cora wants to come out to the theater next week, and I wanted to check with you to see if that's alright." It was the best I could make up on the spot.

"I can't believe you're wasting my time during the day over this. I was in a meeting."

"I'm sorry—"

"We've been over this before. I'm not spending a fortune on a theater ticket if she's not going to remember what she saw five minutes after she gets back on the bus. If I see any charges on our monthly bill for ridiculous extravagances, I'm not going to pay for them. She doesn't need those kinds of things in her life right now. It's not safe for her to be gallivanting around town anyway. What if you lost her? What if she got injured? I don't think you appreciate her state of mind. I don't think you do at all. She needs consistency and familiarity. I saw that she went out for lunch with you last month. If you didn't think I check the bills I get from that place, you're wrong. I do, and I didn't pay for that meal. Why would I pay for her to go out to a restaurant when I've already paid for all her meals in the dining hall there at Gleeful Meadows? Does that sound like something a logical person would do? Does it?"

I wanted to tell her that she was full of crap, and that going out for lunch, and going to museums and the theater and whatever else I felt like dragging her mom along to, was exactly the way that Cora should be spending the last few years of her life.

"And another thing," she continued. "The last time I was there to visit my mom, I saw a candy wrapper in her trash bin. Are you people trying to kill her? She has high blood pressure and is overweight enough as it is. I know you give those candy bars out as bingo prizes, and I'm letting you know right now that if I see one more wrapper anywhere in her room, I'm reporting you to the state. Do you understand that?"

Following my wonderful phone conversation with Cora's daughter, I came out of my office and glanced out the activity room window and saw one of our residents, named Ward B, doing one-handed pushups on the lawn in the courtyard. He was ninety-seven years old, still driving, still dating, and currently going through chemotherapy for a brain tumor. He once voiced how his greatest worry now in life was not that he might die from cancer, but rather that, because of the hair loss from his chemotherapy, women would be turned off by the complete lack of hair on his scrotum.

"I don't like that Wesley Marie," a voice next to me said.

I turned to see Millicent sitting alone in the corner of the activity room. It was unclear to me exactly what Millicent had been doing before I walked out of my office. Daydreaming seemed the likeliest. Her wheelchair was at a peculiar angle, not making it easy for her to join in on any of the activities or conversations with the other ladies, nor to comfortably look out the window or at the fireplace. It was as though someone had gotten fed up with her and just pushed her off to the side.

"Why don't you like Wesley Marie?" I asked.

"She's a busybody," Millicent said.

"Why do you say that?"

"She's always peering over my shoulder to see what I'm doing. I watch her, and I see that she does it to others as well. It's terribly bad manners to always be looking over people's shoulders."

Through the window, I saw Wesley Marie walk up to Ward and stand over him. He didn't notice, or didn't care, or didn't both, and continued with his calisthenics. He stood after completing his pushups and began a series of jumping jacks.

"You couldn't be more wrong about her," I said to Millicent.

"I'm not wrong. I'm a good judge of character, both good and bad characters."

"I'm not supposed to talk about the condition of other residents, but I think it's important you know that Wesley Marie has Alzheimer's disease. She can't control the way she acts. She's in a constant cycle of forgetting and rediscovering. That's why you think she's a busybody. She's curious. Much the same way a baby is. But she won't retain what she learns like a baby does. She'll forget what she's learned and have to rediscover it all over again the next day."

Millicent was silent for a long moment. She turned to look at Wesley Marie, who was now staring at something on the walkway, a spot, or an insect perhaps. Millicent then looked back up at me. "I had no idea."

"How could you?" I asked.

"I'm sorry. I…" Her voice trailed off as she appeared to shut down. I thought she might throw herself onto the floor or try to hit me or scream, but, instead, she just looked at her twisted and crippled hand. Using her other hand, she began trying to straighten the fingers out, first pulling all fingers together, then trying each individually. Their rigidity made me think they would snap off if she applied too much pressure. Spent of will or interest, she stopped, and then scratched a piece of pink nail polish from one of her fingers. "I'm sorry for thinking bad thoughts of her," she said finally, without looking up at me.

"Don't apologize to me," I said.

I thought perhaps this was a turning point with Millicent. She came back from the hospital with a greater ability and desire to acknowledge the needs of those around her and to abide by social etiquette and limitations.

But then the packages started to arrive.

The first shipment came as a surprise to us all. The usual bundle of mail for the community was accompanied by four crates of tiny parcels, all addressed to Millicent, probably about thirty in all. Curious to see what they were, several staff and residents watched as she slowly began to open them at a table in our lounge. Her difficulty moving made it a long and arduous process to even get the first of them open.

"Can I help?" I asked.

"Of course," she said graciously, pushing the parcel to me across the table at which she sat.

I sat down next to her and tore the package open. Inside was a diamond necklace. Millicent smiled as I handed it to her. She watched it sparkle in the firelight. I opened the next and removed a ruby bracelet.

"Oh, my goodness," I said. "Who are they from?"

She let lose a slight chuckle. "I've got no secret admirers, if that's what you're wondering. I ordered the jewelry for myself."

I looked at the postal crates. "There must be dozens of packages," I said. "What are you going to do with so much jewelry?" Some of the nearby ladies were peering with interest at the packages, wondering if, perhaps, they had found themselves on Millicent's gift list.

"I'm going to sell them on eBay."

Hopes were shattered about, perhaps, getting a new brooch or set of earrings for Christmas, and the other ladies moved on to other points of interest.

"You're kidding, right?" I asked.

"Not at all. I've heard that you can make a fortune reselling things on eBay."

"Do you even own a computer?"

"I've ordered one. It's on its way." She continued to stare at the diamond necklace, which she dangled in front of herself. "Open another one," she said.

"I don't know much about jewelry, but it looks like you've spent thousands here."

"I'll get it all back with much more."

"Who gave you this idea?"

"A lady on QVC, the home shopping channel. She said it's a perfect business for seniors and disabled people. That's me on both counts." A sick feeling rose within me.

After recounting the conversation to Paul, Shana had called Doreen, Millicent's daughter-in-law. Doreen was the only person in Millicent's family who could still tolerate Millicent enough to be involved in her daily care. Doreen had known nothing about the jewelry or Millicent's eBay ambitions. As far as she knew, Millicent didn't even own a credit card. As soon as written consent from Doreen arrived, Shana told Millicent that she would keep her jewelry in our safe. She reluctantly turned it all over to her. While that conversation took place, Paul supervised a search of Millicent's room, during which six credit cards were found.

Over the next two weeks, six hundred and twelve more items of jewelry arrived for Millicent. They were each cataloged, stored in the safe, and eventually collected by Doreen and returned to QVC. Not a single further item reached Millicent.

It took her a few weeks to figure out what was happening to her packages. She had a caregiver push her to Paul's office and yelled and screamed, and we all listened and were glad that she took her anger out solely on him. I didn't want her to know that I had had a hand in the arrangement. Even though I was merely looking out for her, my role as friend to the residents made me feel as though, on some level, I had betrayed her.

Millicent proved to be a clever and resourceful challenge to our efforts to keep her from completely bankrupting her family with her money-making scheme through eBay jewelry sales. She continued receiving letters from various banks and financial institutions, in which the outline of a new credit card could be felt through the envelope. These were all forwarded to Doreen, who would then cancel them. Bank after bank sent credit cards to Millicent, and, somehow, one of them slipped through our dragnet. There was a rapid burst of jewelry-filled packages that followed soon after, before that credit card, too, was confiscated and cancelled.

Doreen then cancelled Millicent's phone connection, which was the catalyst to Millicent's subsequent constant, relentless pursuing of me to drive her to the bank and the library. She claimed her desire to go to the library was so she could do some research on the origins of a painting she had once purchased in Bangladesh. I decided that paranoia was a good policy and assumed that she really just wanted to go to the library to use their computers to order more credit cards.

I wondered how Doreen, not being a blood relative, could continue to put herself through the frustration of acting as Millicent's power of attorney. She never wavered in her love and support of Millicent and her desire to do what was best for her, no matter how difficult Millicent made things for Doreen.

Then Doreen did something unexpected. She died.

Doreen had battled breast cancer for the past year, though her own pain and suffering had never showed. It was always eclipsed by Millicent and her needs. There was now no one other than us to protect Millicent from herself, since both her children wanted nothing to do with her. Millicent's response to the news of Doreen's passing was subdued. I found it difficult to believe that she didn't care for Doreen in the way that Doreen had cared for her, but Millicent was one of those people who the rest of us would say "showed their love and appreciation in ways we can't quite understand."

As I parked the bus next to the front entrance of Gleeful Meadows, Muana, one of our caregivers, got to her feet and began unstrapping Millicent and her wheelchair. Millicent awoke and looked around. "What's going on? Where am I?" she asked.

"You were just at Doreen's funeral," Muana said.

"Yes. Yes, of course." The moment Millicent had fallen asleep on the ride home had been a blessing for me, as it meant she stopped insisting that I park the bus at the bank so she could "say hello to an old friend."

I stood and pushed the overhead button that opened the side door to the bus. As soon as the rubber seals on the doors parted, we could hear the sound of raised voices. I took my finger off the button and turned back toward Millicent and Muana, who were both craning their necks, looking for the source of the voices. Around the corner of the building, I could see a human shadow.

"I don't care what you think you're entitled to." I recognized this as Paul's voice. "You come back on the property again, and I'm going to have you arrested. You put a hand on your old man again, and I'm going to punch your teeth in."

"You lay a hand on me, and I'll sue you," another voice said.

"You lay a hand on your old man again, and you won't be around to sue anybody."

"That's James F's son," I said to Millicent and Muana.

"Oh, he's such a sweet boy," Millicent said.

"Not that son. The other one. The drunk one," I said.

"It's not right for us to be listening in on their conversation," Muana said.

"We're not listening. They just happen to be talking where we can hear them," I said.

"Shush," Millicent said. "I can't hear."

Raymond F staggered around the side of the building and leaned his hand up against the bus. He began scraping the bottom of his shoe on the edge of the bumper. Paul came into view and watched Raymond from the corner of the building. Neither of them could see us through the tinted bus windows. Millicent peered down at the top of Raymond's head, which was just on the other side of the glass from her. Large aviator shades were perched atop his shiny head.

He turned back to Paul. "Big man," he said.

"Get going."

Raymond walked to his Harley, stumbled, and then straddled the bike. The engine came to life with a terrible rumble. He pulled a flask from his breast pocket, took a swig, and then repocketed it. He turned back to Paul, flipped him the bird, and then roared out of the parking lot.

"What was that all about?" I asked.

"Yesterday he was here and demanded money from James," Millicent said. "James said he wasn't going to give him any until he sobered up. Arnold D then went into the room and said he'd call the police if Raymond didn't leave."

Unfortunately, Raymond was one of those family members who saw senior care as nothing more than a fancy way for their inheritance to diminish. I later found out, partially from Millicent, that Raymond had been on the outs from his family for the last several years and had no interest in reconnecting with either his father or his brother, Marty. That is, until Raymond learned that every spare penny his father had ever saved had been wisely invested and, over the years, had become a small fortune. Marty had control over James's finances and used the money to pay for a comfortable life for his old man. Raymond saw this as a waste of the money, rationalizing that their old man hadn't lived well previously in life, so why should he start now?

Before Raymond had completely thrown himself back into their lives, he had managed to drain over a hundred thousand dollars from his father's savings account without Marty's knowledge. The Harley Davidson that he had just peeled away on was bought with that stolen money.

As soon as I entered the reception area with Millicent and Muana, Iris came up to me. "I can't stand that lady. She's so strange."

"Who?" I asked.

She pointed outside to Wesley Marie, who was looking in on us with her hands and face pressed up against the glass. "That one."

"What did she do?"

"She's doing it right now. She's just been staring in at us for the past hour. Do you know how unsettling that is?"

"Did you go ask her if she'd like to come in and join you?"

"Now why would I do that?"

"It's a friendly thing to do."

"I'm not her friend."

As Iris gestured wildly with her arms, my attention drifted to a woman who sat in the corner of the room. She had been left there by her son about three hours ago. The woman did not live at Gleeful Meadows, nor did her son make an appointment to view the property. They simply walked in arm-in-arm, he sat her on the sofa, and then left. We had tried to find out who the woman was and if she knew when, or if ever, her son would come back for her. She was either extremely shy or extremely demented, as she would not respond to our attempts at communication. Come to think of it, we didn't even know if she spoke English.

Iris faded from my thoughts as I watched this woman watch the rest of us in the room. She hadn't eaten or drank anything since she had been here. Her eyes moved to look at Wesley Marie at the window. Had she noticed her because of her odd behavior, or had she been drawn to her as a kindred demented spirit?

"It's not her fault," a voice said behind me.

I turned and saw that the voice was Millicent's.

"Pardon me?" I asked.

"She's complaining about Wesley Marie," Millicent said, gesturing to Iris.

"So what if I am?" Iris said.

"It's not her fault the way she acts. She can't help it. She's sick, and you need to have compassion for her."

I stared at Millicent with disbelief at her ability and willingness to advocate for someone other than herself. Iris threw her hands at us in a gesture of frustration and resignation to a world in which everyone was crazy except for her.

A short time later, as I was preparing for bingo, Elsie wheeled herself over to me. "Can I talk to you for a moment?"

"Of course, Elsie," I said.

She leaned forward and clasped a hand next to her mouth. "In private?"

I nodded, and we walked over to the corner of the activities room. I pulled out a chair and sat next to her. "What's wrong?" I asked.

"It's hard for me to say this. I don't want to cause trouble for anyone."

"What is it?"

"You know the pregnant lady? The one whose room is next to mine." She was talking about Wesley Marie. She had clearly mistaken Wesley Marie's belly for something else. "I don't think she's quite right in the head," Elsie continued. "I wouldn't be saying anything, but I'm worried about her. She also scares me. She comes into my room at night to tuck me in. She also checks on me when I'm in the shower. She comes and gets me for meals and activities, but always at the wrong times. Sometimes, she'll take me away halfway through dinner. She just takes hold of my wheelchair and pushes me along. I don't have the heart to tell her that she's got her times all mixed up. I also don't have the heart to tell her just to leave me alone. I know she's trying to be kind, but it really frightens me."

I inhaled deeply and exhaled as slowly as I could before answering. "Wesley Marie will be moving away very soon."

"Goodness, no. I said I didn't want to get anyone in trouble. Please, just forget what I've said." Elsie put her hand on my knee and squeezed.

"You didn't get her in trouble. Her move was already planned," I said.

"You're just saying that so I don't feel guilty."

"Elsie, you have nothing to feel guilty about. We have to look out for each other here. If someone saw that you were in pain, wouldn't you want that person to tell someone?"

"It's not the same thing."

"It's exactly the same thing. Wesley Marie needs more care now, and I'm glad you came to tell me what you've noticed. It helps us give her the proper care that she needs."

That night, Wesley Marie woke up just after two and went for a walk off the property. If she hadn't been noticed by a staff member arriving for the night shift, who knows where she would have ended up? Wesley Marie wasn't seen again by the residents in assisted living. She was immediately taken to her new room, behind the safety of the locked doors of the Family Circle.

Most of the residents in assisted living were afraid of the residents in the Family Circle. Not because they saw them as violent or frightening, but because they saw too much of themselves in them. Many of the Family Circle residents had once lived in assisted living before their dementia became dangerous to their own safety. The assisted living residents knew that it could also happen to any of them, and that there was no return.

Sadly, Wesley Marie declined quickly once she moved into the Family Circle, as she no longer had access to the routines that gave her life meaning and some semblance of stability. There was a small grouping of flowers in the memory care courtyard, but they didn't pull her interest like those on the rest of the property. All things that grew there had to be edible, as many of the demented residents took any opportunity to put something into their mouths. Wesley Marie could also no longer go out for her morning walk to Starbucks, so she had to give up her grande Americano for the decaffeinated, lukewarm drip that the Family Circle offered. She spent her days walking in the courtyard, always alone.

One evening, soon after her move, a friend of hers came to visit. Wesley Marie's family came often, but I was thankful that she still had friends who held her in their hearts and prayers.

"Wesley Marie and I have known each other since college. We were sorority sisters," the woman said, as I walked her to Wesley Marie's room.

"That's wonderful. I know she'll be so happy to see you," I said.

I knocked on her door. After a moment, the door opened, and Wesley Marie looked out at us.

She smiled and, in her even, steady voice said, "Theresa, I see you've found Kevin."

"He was kind enough to show me the way."

"Come in." Wesley Marie stepped to the side to allow her friend to enter.

Minutes later, as I surfed the internet at the front desk, Theresa passed toward the front exit. "That was a quick visit," I said.

She turned to me. "I couldn't look at her any longer. She's not the person I knew." Theresa removed a tissue from her purse and blotted the space below each of her eyes. She looked back in the direction she had just come as though she expected to see someone or something pursuing her.

"What do you mean?" I asked, already knowing what her response would be.

"She smelled like she had soiled herself. She spilled wine all over her blouse, and, in the middle of our conversation, she started reading the newspaper. I don't think I can visit again. I'll write, but I don't think I can see her again like that. Not like that."

"You're being incredibly selfish. Is this how you would act visiting a loved one in the hospital with terminal cancer? More concerned about how it makes *you* feel? Wesley Marie needs friendship and support, not people pitying themselves because they can't relive the past like they had hoped. Get over yourself and get back in there."

That's what I wanted to say, but I didn't. I told her I understood, because, deep down, below where sentiment clouds rational thought, I knew I did understand how she felt. Before she left, she again assured me that she would write.

To my knowledge, she never sent a single letter.

To this day, I'm conflicted about that night. Alzheimer's frightens people in a way that only diseases of the mind can. The fear of losing one's mind is so palpable that to confront it in another, a loved one, can sometimes be too much to handle. But is that an excuse? Shouldn't our love for that person overshadow irrational fears about our own mortality? I don't know. I can't judge the way someone else acts in a situation that I've never experienced. I wanted to shake that woman for putting her own needs before those of Wesley Marie, but, at the same time, I wanted to hug her, to thank her for the friendship she had given Wesley Marie thus far. I don't know if my anger that night was based more on my own affection for Wesley Marie or a desire to protect her from hurt arising from that affection.

I just don't know.

CHAPTER NINE

Mixed Nuts

"A few years ago, as soon as I got off the plane back in Vancouver for a visit from Australia, I went with my mom, on a ferry, over to Victoria to visit a great aunt of mine who was in the hospital. We had been told that this was it, that she'd be a goner any day now. It was your typical hospital visit—awkward small talk with the person you're visiting, hugs all around, and then you're gone.

"Anyway, that great aunt finally passed away a couple of days ago, and over the weekend, my mom called and told me that I'm credited with giving her those last few years of her life. Apparently, so the family lore now recounts, she was so touched by my visit, not my mom's, or any of the other countless people who came to see her, but mine alone—she was so touched by it that she was brought back from the brink of death to live in health and happiness for another couple of years, until she was finally struck dead by a massive heart attack."

"You're making this up," Bernice said.

"I wish I was. I didn't ask to have the power to heal. It's a tremendous responsibility," I said.

"Oh stop."

"I would if I could, but, apparently, these hands are like those that brought Lazarus back from the dead."

"Why are you so silly?" someone asked.

"Does your mom believe that cock and bull story?" Cora asked.

"No, she knows that I'm useless at most things. Especially miraculous revival."

"I saw somebody die once," Dorothea said. "One minute she was telling me that she had gas, and the next minute she was gone. You can tell right away, you know."

"What do you mean you can tell?" Bernice asked. "Of course, you can tell. They're not breathing anymore."

"It's more than that. They're not there anymore. It's like they're just a shell. Their soul is gone, and you can tell."

"Angie's told me something similar," I said. "She's seen a lot of dead people, some right after they've passed, and she said that they look different right away."

"Why are we talking about this?" Dorothea asked.

"You started it," I said.

"Well now I'm finishing it."

Following the miraculous healing and soulless corpse talk, I took a group of residents to IHOP for lunch. As per usual, immediately after we ordered, several residents forgot we had just done so and started to complain that we hadn't yet ordered. I told them that I had taken the liberty of ordering for them ahead of our arrival. Then, when the food arrived, a chorus of complaints began about how obscenely large the portion sizes were and how ridiculous the prices must also be. Then, when the bill came, most residents frisked themselves for their wallets and then asked who was going to pay for the meal. My usual reply, which never grew old because no one could remember it anyway, was that we'd be working off the cost of our meals in the kitchen.

Upon our return to Gleeful Meadows, I was summoned to the beauty shop twice within a half-hour period to help transfer residents from the stylist's chair into wheelchairs. The first was Norma B, who was blind, deaf, and mostly paralyzed. It broke my heart when, while the stylist and I were lifting her, Norma referred to herself in the third person and sadly commented that she was good for nothing. After that, I was called upon to help transfer Henrietta, whose latest psychosomatic ailment was that she had forgotten how to walk. As soon as we hoisted her to her feet, she pooped in her pants, and the beauty shop had to be shut down for the rest of the day to air out. The stylist then said she refused to come back to work until the care staff took the initiative to scrape the feces from beneath the fingernails of the Family Circle residents before they were brought to the salon for their manicures.

As I left the salon, I saw Tom standing in front of the reception desk, waiting for service. Jennifer was not there, so I walked up behind him. "What can I do for you, Tom?"

"You look like the man for the job. I need to get a hold of my social security number. I can't seem to find my card, and I can't seem to remember my number."

"We've got all that information on file. What did you need it for?"

"This fellow on the phone needs it."

"What fellow?"

"Not sure that I can remember."

"I hate to say it, Tom, but this is exactly the reason why we're holding your social security card for you."

"You think this fellow was trying to hoodwink me?"

"Is he still on the line?"

I followed Tom back to his room. His phone receiver rested on his nightstand, out of its cradle. I sat on his bed and picked up the receiver. There was silence on the other end. Then I heard a sigh. "Who's there?" I asked. There was a click as the person hung up.

A month earlier, a newspaper canvasser had somehow gotten a list of our resident's phone numbers and signed most of them up for yearly subscriptions. He had told them each that the subscription was a gift from their children, then got the children's phone numbers from the residents and told the children that their mom or dad had called the paper and asked for a subscription. Credit card numbers were flying over the phone lines. Who wouldn't want to make Mom or Dad happy with a little daily reading?

The elderly were a goldmine for the unscrupulous.

During my lunch break, I interviewed a woman named Cynthia for a position as an activities volunteer. She had brought her three-year-old daughter with her, who was sitting happily next to her mom on the sofa reading a book. The interview was going splendidly, and I knew that Cynthia and her daughter would make excellent visitors for our residents. After I photocopied her driver's license, I handed it back to her, and again sat down in my chair.

"I hope you don't mind," she said to me.

"Not at all," I responded, without knowing what she was referring to.

As we began to talk again, I noticed that her daughter was no longer next to her. I looked around the room to see if the little girl had snuck off for some mischief or to look around, but she was nowhere in sight. I looked back at Cynthia, and it finally registered that she had covered herself with a blanket, and her daughter's legs stuck out from underneath. For the rest of the interview, she proceeded to breastfeed the little girl, and I had to fight with all my will to not let my eye line fall below Cynthia's face.

Following the interview, I took them on a short tour of the community, during which I introduced them to several residents. As we moved through the hall of the Family Circle, Cynthia's little girl dropped the cookie she had been chewing. Frances, who had been following us, while telling us about the invisible dog who was following her, bent quickly down and retrieved the cookie. Before she could hand the cookie back to the little girl, I snatched it away from her. Instead of explaining about poopy fingers and risking scaring Cynthia away forever, I simply explained that, in healthcare facilities across the world, the five-second rule for food dropped on the floor did not exist.

I looked up at the clock. It was finally time to set up the activity room for the performance of our play.

The turnout was remarkable. Most of the residents from our assisted living floors had come to watch the performance, and most of the Family Circle residents who could be trusted to sit through the performance without getting up to wander or start suddenly screaming uncontrollably, and who could maintain control of their bodily functions for reasonable durations, were escorted in to watch. Most touching were the family members of residents who had taken time off from work to come and watch their mom or dad or grandparent in the performance.

At the front of the room sat our cast, in a row of chairs facing the audience, each with a placard hung around their necks displaying the name of their character. To the left were residents who were acting as our sound-effect technicians, and to the right were those who were in charge of the light switches and the musical interlude—by way of a xylophone and a harmonica.

The rear doors into the room opened, and a large group of seniors whom I did not recognize entered. In the process of finding places for them all to sit, I learned that they were from another assisted living facility and had come to watch our activity as an activity on their own calendar.

After a brief introduction by me, Grace lowered the lights, as Leona began rockin' out on her harmonica, and a woman named Audrey D accompanied on the xylophone.

Using blocks of wood attached to a rusty hinge and platform shoes on top of a table, our residents in charge of sound effects began to create the scene for the rest of us. Then Cora as Molly and Sol as Fibber began the show.

CORA: Did you mail that letter?

SOL: Why, Molly! Am I the kind of a guy who, when you tell him to do something you want done, he don't do it?

CORA: McGee! Did you mail that letter or not?

SOL: No.

The audience laughed, and I thought to myself that this might actually turn out to be a success. As long as neither Iris or Cora suddenly forgot they were in a performance and got up to go the restroom, no one forgot that Hazel was deaf and needed to be elbowed when it was time for her lines, and Mildred didn't get frustrated with the other performers and punch someone.

What could possibly go wrong?

SOL: ...But I'll mail your letter right away. Should o' done it yesterday! Sorry I forgot, but you can consider the error rectified!

SOUND: Door opens.

SOL: I'll just dash across the street to the mailbox, Molly. Be right back!

SOUND: Footsteps on steps...sidewalk...then... Elsie smacked a large plunger against a wall and then pulled it away creating a great big suctioning sound that reverberated throughout the room.

CORA: Oh no, Fibber! Someone, help. He's stuck in that fresh pavement.

Now it was Dorothea who had her moment to shine. I saw the stage fright leave her body as she got to her feet. Her daughter in the front row began taking photographs of her mother as tears streamed down her face.

DOROTHEA: I know what to do. Get a couple shovels!...see? Then, go down into the basement of your house...Dig a tunnel till you're right under him...Then dig up till you reach him and pull him down through!

Again, the audience erupted with laughter. I looked at the faces and the joy they displayed. There was no disability in this room. There was no cancer, no Alzheimer's, and no death lurking in the corner waiting to prey. It was as though we were in attendance at a school play, with child performers, who had their lives ahead of, not merely behind, them.

As I was looking at the faces in the dimly lit room, I saw one of the residents from the other assisted living facility and thought she looked familiar. I made my way to her. Could it be her? No.

"Are you Lily?" I whispered as I sat next to her.

"Yes, I remember you too," she said as she turned to look at me. "You were always kind, so I don't forget."

It was Lily L, the holocaust survivor, whose daughter had moved her from Gleeful Meadows after we had continually dropped the ball when it came to her care. The difference in her appearance and expression was extraordinary. She had put on about forty pounds of healthy weight. She no longer looked like a pathetic waif. But the personality she displayed was what I found hardest to believe. She laughed and joked with the people around her.

During our conversation, I learned that, for several years before she moved to our community, she had been overmedicated, close to the point of being a walking zombie. When she moved into Gleeful Meadows, our intake assessor hadn't questioned the doses that she was on. Perhaps, at one point in her life, she needed to be that far removed from the world around her. But no longer. Thankfully, someone had realized that and dialed back her meds, allowing the woman she had once been to emerge again.

When her daughter had finally moved her out of our care at Gleeful Meadows, I had felt a sense of sadness. I had wanted her to stay. However, seeing how she had changed, I was glad she had left. Whatever we had not been able to do for her, I was glad to see that others could. She was happy.

I turned my attention back to the play.

MILDRED: What's that guy doing out there in the street? Advertising something?

IRIS: No, they say he got stuck in that fresh pavement.

MILDRED: Well, if he saw they were going to pave the street, why didn't he get out of the way?

SOL: Hey, Molly! Molly!

CORA: Yes, dearie…here I am! And here's a little footstool for you to sit on…catch!

SOUND: Mimicking the cartoonish sound of an object being thrown through the air, Ken put two fingers in his mouth and whistled so loud that even Hazel heard it without her hearing aids turned on and began looking around the room.

MILDRED: Hey, stick-in-the-mud!!...Can I have your autograph?

SOL: Why certainly, bud! Throw me your death certificate!

IRIS: Say...you're in a tough spot, pal! Can't you pull yourself loose?

SOL: Who, me? Why, sure. I'm just standin' here till the steam roller comes by. Then I'll lie down and get my pants pressed.

"Sollie," a shrill voice screamed from the back of the room. Everyone turned to see Henrietta, Sol's wife, who had just been escorted into the room by a caregiver. Sol halted mid sentence and stared at his estranged wife. He made an effort to get to his feet but fell back into his chair. Henrietta rushed to the front of the room and positioned herself between Sol and Cora.

"Sollie, dear, who's this woman?" Henrietta asked. "Is she the reason why you've been kept from me? Did you know that they wouldn't let me see you?" She sat in his lap, threw her arms around him, and kissed his cheeks furiously. "Oh, my goodness, I'm so glad we're finally together again. I don't know who this woman is, but I don't want you seeing her again. Sollie, look at me when I'm talking to you. We're meant to be together forever. Our children are counting on us to set the right example for them. Now that we're back together, we can get our lives back to the way they were before we came to this awful place."

Sol looked for the nearest exit, and once it was in view, he pushed Henrietta off of him and walked as quickly as he could toward it.

Henrietta moved to intercept him, but Shana stood in her way. "Look at those gorgeous earrings you've got. I want to get a pair just like them." Henrietta pushed Shana aside and reached the door just as it slammed shut in her face.

The room on the other side of the door, our staff room, had no other exit. Henrietta attempted to turn the knob, which wouldn't move, presumably because Sol was holding tightly onto it from the other side, as though his life depended upon it. Perhaps it truly did.

"I want to see my husband," Henrietta screamed. By then, a swarm of care staff had gathered around her in an attempt to divert her attention long enough that she would forget about having just run into Sol, or, at the very least, long enough so that Sol could come back out through the door and find an exit that actually went somewhere.

Mildred began pounding her fist on the nearest table and directed all her pent-up frustration toward the family members who sat in the audience, shocked by the spectacle, "You see what we have to live with? You see what goes on here on a daily basis? You see how this place is one stroke short of a cuckoo clock?"

As though in an attempt to give Sol the diversion he so desperately needed, or merely to prove Mildred right, Audrey D wheeled past me and grabbed the mask I had made for my role in the play as a dog, put it on, and began barking and shouting, "Look at me, I'm Kevin, the doggie. Woof, woof, woof."

An hour later, I had just finished cleaning up the activity room and was taking a garbage bag out the front door to the dumpster, when Bernice came up to me. Her Chihuahua named Drywall was perched upon the crossbeam of her walker. Six years earlier, when Bernice and her late husband, Henry, had moved back into their newly remodeled condo, they heard a rustling sound while they lay in bed trying to sleep. Upon searching the house with baseball bat and tennis racket in hand, they discovered that the sound was coming from within one of the newly completed walls. Henry put his ear to the wall and heard scratching and whimpering. Rather than wait until morning to call the contractor, he retrieved a crowbar from his car trunk and ripped a hole in the wall behind which they found an emaciated Chihuahua. Next to the dog was a litter of dead baby pups. Bernice and Henry later learned that the dog had belonged to one of the carpenters who had worked on the house. He had brought the dog to work one day, and the dog had vanished. In reality, she had sought out a place to give birth to her babies within the wall, and had been sealed in when the drywall had been put up. Bernice remembered the man whom the dog had belonged to and decided that he probably didn't take very good care of her and, in spite of Henry's protests, Bernice had decided to keep her.

"When's bingo?" Bernice asked.

"Tomorrow," I said.

"Tomorrow? What am I supposed to do until then?"

"How about whittling a baseball bat out of a tree trunk and hitting me over the head with it."

"Are you down about something?"

"How could you tell?"

"I think you need a hug," she said.

I put down the bag of trash and turned to her with my arms spread wide.

Bernice took a step back. "Not from me, buster."

"Why won't you give me a hug, Bernice? You're the only resident here who consistently refuses to give me a hug. Who doesn't like hugs?"

"I like hugs just fine. I just don't want to hug you."

"Why not?"

"You're too fat."

"Holy crap. Did you just actually say that to me?"

"You were so much thinner when you started working here. What happened to you?"

"It's baby weight."

"You're wife's the one who's pregnant, not you."

"It's sympathy weight."

"Well, you're not getting any sympathy hugs from me."

I took another step toward Bernice with my arms spread wide. She picked up a wooden skewer off of the food table behind her and jabbed me in the stomach with it. "You get away from me, you fatty," she said as she grabbed her walker and ran to the other side of the room. I was amazed at how fast Bernice could move once she had her hands on the reins of her walker.

"I'll get a hug from you one of these days," I said.

Following the abrupt ending of our performance, we had served cocktails to the residents and their family members. Dorothea got drunk and spilled her martini. When Paul said that she'd had too much and should probably go lie down in her room, she insisted that she wasn't going anywhere until someone replaced the half of her martini that had ended up on the floor.

I had looked around the room at the people laughing and talking, and a few who were even dancing, and I was reminded of why I had fallen in love with the world of senior care in the first place. These were people who knew just how fleeting health, happiness, and even life, were. Some of them, like Mildred and Adeline, were victims of their afflictions and sorrows. But the majority had learned that there is no choice in life but to move on, to truly put those things behind you that get in the way of living the life you have left.

As I was filling up my coffee mug, the phone at the reception desk began to ring, and, as usual, Jennifer was nowhere in sight. I reached over the desk and picked up the receiver.

"Kevin, it's Adeline. Could you have someone look into the third floor hallway to see if that new gal is still there pacing?"

"Who?"

"I don't know what her name is. She's old like the rest of us."

"Why don't you just pop your head out your door?" I asked.

"Because then I might have to talk to her. She's nuts."

"That's not a very nice thing to say."

"Sometimes the truth isn't pretty."

I thought about telling Adeline the truth about her not-so-pretty camel toe, created by the only pair of pants she owned, or about how every time she opened her mouth and I got a look at her three remaining teeth, one of which was currently stained orange, I wanted to barf. But, instead, I just said, "I'll go see if she's there."

When I stepped out from the elevator, I saw Judith R with her arms akimbo, looking down the hallway like a high school hall monitor. I walked alongside of her. Judith had a large, bulbous nose and fat earlobes and gave the impression she had jumped right off of the page of a caricaturist's drawing. She turned to look at me with deep-set creases on her brow.

"Whatcha looking for?" I asked.

"Waiting for my no-good husband. He's been out all night and hasn't called once to tell me he's not dead or been in a car wreck."

"He might have left a message at the front desk. Perhaps someone just forgot to give it to you."

She looked at me suspiciously. "Aren't you the one having a baby?"

"My wife is, yes."

"Are you a no-good two-timer?"

"Um, no, I'm not, Judith."

"Because when that little one comes along, you're going to have to be there for your family. No running out on them. You understand that?"

"Yes."

"I've got two little ones myself, and that husband of mine should know better than to leave us all alone."

There were many things I didn't understand about the dementia I was confronted with on a daily basis. Sometimes, talking with a demented resident was like being in a strong gust of wind. The more you resisted the reality they presented you with, the more likely you were to get knocked down by them. Literally.

On the other hand, if you walked the journey with them, not fighting the strong gusts that threatened to carry you away, the more likely both of you were to come out of the conversation on the far side with smiles on your faces. I wondered how her reality could allow her both to be living in an assisted living facility (she acknowledged that we had a front desk person) and yet, at the same time, believe she's still raising her two young children and that her husband is still alive. Pursuing my curiosity with her would not only be cruel, it would be fruitless, I suspected. We would both end up confused, only her confusion would likely leave her hurt and more alone than merely being an eighty-year-old woman with two grown children living on the other side of the country and a husband who's been dead since the Second World War.

I walked to the phone on the wall and dialed the front desk.

Jennifer answered. "Front desk."

"Hi, Jennifer, this is Kevin. Judith would like to know if her husband has called for her."

"Her husband? Is she married?"

"Oh, he did," I said. "Wonderful."

"What?" Jennifer asked.

"And what time did he say he'd be back?"

"What's wrong with you?" Jennifer said before hanging up the phone.

I kept the receiver to my face for several more moments. "Alright, I'll tell her. Thank you." I hung up the phone. Judith looked at me expectedly. "He called about an hour ago. He's stuck in traffic on the other side of the pass. He's going to be late but wanted you to know that he's alright."

When I got down to the front desk, Jennifer was taking an inquiry call, and I didn't feel like waiting it out to fill her in on the common sense parts of the conversation that she had missed. I turned around and was met by Tom, who, even hunched over his walker, was still taller than me.

"Are you the fellow who organizes the walking team?"

"Hi, Tom. Yes, we'll be leaving in about fifteen minutes."

"Do I have time to try out for the team?"

"You don't need to try out for it. It's just a group, not a team."

Tom pushed himself upright, let go of his walker, and shuffled sideways away from it. "Look at me, I'm walking, I'm walking."

I grabbed Tom and supported his weight. "Are you crazy?" I asked.

"I had to show you that I could walk."

"Okay, you made the team," I said as I shuffled him back over to his walker.

He grabbed hold of it and then clapped me on the shoulder. "When do we set off?"

"Fourteen minutes."

I had spent most of the day avoiding Cora. If I saw her making her way toward me down a hallway, I turned around and found another route to my destination. This was one of the perks of having much better vision than most of the residents—like a shark, I saw them a long time before they saw me. For the past few days, Cora had been taking antibiotics for a urinary tract infection. The symptoms of many illnesses are different for seniors than they are for the rest of the population. For a middle-aged adult, the symptoms of a UTI would be along the lines of burning and discomfort when urinating. With a senior, it caused temporary delirium. This, thankfully, made the possible presence of a UTI easier to spot in the senior population—that is, assuming the senior in question was reasonably sound of mind to begin with. One day they're fine; the next day they're nuts.

My first introduction to this phenomenon was when Grace came and told me that she had left all her laundry at her daughter-in-law's house. I called the daughter-in-law and was told that Grace had never brought laundry over and, yet, had been calling her every ten minutes all day and jabbering on about mismatched socks, separating the lights from the darks, and fabric softener that gave her hives. As we were on speaker phone, at the mention of hives, Grace pulled up her sweater to show me her boob, and I turned away just before the nipple appeared and said hello. A week later, following a course of antibiotics, Grace was back to her usual self, with her laundry in her room, exactly where it had always been.

A similar episode had now happened with Cora. She had already been diagnosed with a urinary tract infection and was being treated, and all we had to do in the meantime was ride out the worst of her personality change. Unfortunately, that personality change had pulled a chair up in front of my office door and sat itself down. I needed to get in there.

"Oh, Kevin, I'm so glad you're here. I need your help," Cora said.

I tried to squeeze past her, but her head blocked the doorknob. "I just have to make a phone call, Cora, and then, after that, I need to run out for a doctor's appointment."

"That little Spanish girl is still in my room," she said.

Not this again, oh please, not this again, I thought.

"I know Cora, but perhaps the caregivers would be the best ones to help you out with that. I think I hear my phone ringing." I tried to turn the knob, but I couldn't as her wig had wrapped itself around it.

"They don't believe me that she's there. Right now, she's hiding under my sink. When one of the caregivers came in to check, the little girl hid under the bed so that they couldn't find her."

"I'm sure she's gone by now. Why don't you go check, and then call me on my office phone if you see her?"

"By the time you come over, she might be hiding someplace else. I don't speak Spanish, so I don't know what she wants or why she's hiding in my room. She might be hungry or hurt."

"I don't speak Spanish either."

Our walking group set out with its greatest number to date. There were twenty of us, with Tom taking up the rear. "How about you make a little room for me in your lap," he said to Elsie as she wheeled past him in her chair.

I was glad to get out into the fresh air, away from the staleness of the building. There was a cool breeze, which came at us through the trees from the neighboring forest. A deer watched us as we made our way along the side of the building, laughing and joking about the spectacle that had occurred during the earlier performance. I knew I was going to miss these days and these people. I hadn't yet told them I was leaving. My job had a different expectation than most. That of friend. Leaving it was as though I was taking my friendship with me. Or at least that's how it seemed to me. That was the thought that was running through my head when I heard the clanging of metal against pavement, followed by a thump. I turned to see Tom lying next to his overturned walker. He wasn't moving.

CHAPTER TEN

The Storm

Leona P was a source of continual fascination for me. She was tough and witty, more macho than I, could play the harmonica, broke into random sermons for no other reason than to spread the gospel, loved poetry, and was, most likely, mentally and physically abusive to her husband Lloyd. Lloyd and I had gotten off to a bad start. He had kicked my cat on the first day I had met him, and I sternly told him not to do it again. The words unsaid, but implied by my tone, were that I would shove my shoe so far up his ass that he'd have to open his mouth for me to tie my laces.

Lloyd almost never spoke. He had suffered a stroke several years earlier and was slow in movement, voice, and thought. However, after watching this dynamic duo for the six months that they resided at Gleeful Meadows, I came to the conclusion that Lloyd's faculties were not as impaired as he let on. I came to believe that he feigned such a level of handicap to avoid both conflict and conversation with Leona. However, I never called him out on this, as he was never far from the side of Leona, whom I also would never want to piss off. As Lloyd's caregiver, from spoon feeding him to wiping his behind, Leona had suffered two heart attacks, three ulcers, and countless other setbacks to her health and life from the stress. But she bore it all and went back for more. They were farm folk, like most of the residents at Gleeful Meadows, and as such, much, much tougher than me.

The first day of the storm dropped eighteen inches of snow on Gleeful Meadows and the surrounding area. Like most people, those of us at Gleeful Meadows were caught by surprise, and most of our outdoor furniture was destroyed, some by falling trees and debris, and others were thrown by gusts of wind into the sides of the building.

Angie wanted me to stay home from work, worried that my twenty-mile drive held too many untold dangers for me to attempt the trip. I refused to stay home, so she packed supplies in case my car got stuck and I needed to make a home of it for a while: blankets, warm clothes, bottles of water, and granola bars. What a sweetie.

The ditches along the highway were littered with cars. The snow and ice became thicker as I got closer to Gleeful Meadows. The moisture in the ground from the rains of the weeks before, and the weight of the previous night's snow, had combined to topple trees, pulling up roots and rot, cratering the earth around us. A local gas station had been destroyed by an old, tall evergreen, which had finally lost its life to this storm. Its branches were blown from its trunk, salting the air and pavement for miles.

Before pulling into the driveway at work, I already could have guessed which staff members would not be at work that day: the clock watchers. The power was out in most of the county, so perhaps their alarm clocks just hadn't gone off.

Instead of a bleak start to the day, however, the residents were greeted with whimsy. Leona had awoken early and gone outside into the cold to get to work. When the residents entered the dining hall, they each had a large snowball with cold peas and carrots for a face waiting for them on their breakfast plate. Their real breakfasts weren't much better.

I drove to Safeway and bought forty bags of ice, filling every inch of my tiny car. Then we (and by we, I mean I) loaded the ice into our main walk-in freezer and fridge. Luckily, I had gotten to Safeway before the rest of the city figured on doing the exact same thing. Depending upon how long the blackout lasted, the food would eventually spoil, but we would need as much of it as possible to last as long as possible.

Eric, our chef, couldn't get in to work, so the cooking duties fell upon Paul and Tamara, Eric's assistant, who got to work on the propane grills, making vats of soup, hot cocoa, and coffee. Then, all the residents were brought into the activity room, which was the largest indoor gathering place we had. The chairs and benches and sofas and walkers and wheelchairs were all full and closely packed together. Before long, our body warmth heated the room, and most people seemed to be in relatively good spirits, with the exception of the usual complainers.

"Why don't we have backup generators?"

"Are we going to be compensated for the food that we've paid for?"

"Why don't they turn on the lights?"

There were enough service staff who didn't show up for work to make the serving of soup and hot beverages by the rest of us a continuous day-long event. The cleaning of broken glass and mangled patio equipment would have to wait until everyone was fed and warm.

The landlines were down, so staff members called from their own cell phones to try and reach our residents' family members to first let them know that their loved one was alright, and second, to ask if they could come get them. We were able to pawn a few residents off onto sons, daughters, or spouses, whose houses either still had power or, at least, had a backup generator. We all knew that the inevitable question once this was all over would be: "So am I going to be financially compensated for taking in my father when I was already paying you guys to look after him?"

Winter is a bad time for many seniors, even when surrounded by warmth and happiness. Winter seems to claim more elderly lives than its fair share. No one said it, but we all worried about the cold, dark nights ahead of us and how many of our residents those nights would claim. Perhaps even our residents were wondering the same thing: afraid, or perhaps relieved, that their time to let go of this world might soon be upon them.

"My phone doesn't work." I turned to see Norris Q standing next to me.

"It's because of the blackout," I said.

"What blackout?" Norris was blind and, therefore, used to walking around in the dark.

"The storm's knocked out the power for most of the county."

"Oh, come now. You're just pulling my leg."

"Yes, Norris, I'm just pulling your leg."

Norris pretended to look around the room. He squinted and moved his face closer to mine. "You know, come to think of it, it does seem a little darker."

"We turned 'em off, trying to cut down on our electricity bill."

"So no TV?"

"No."

"What am I supposed to do without TV?"

"Do you just listen to it?"

"Of course, I just listen. What else would I do, lick the static off the screen?"

"Ha! Static off the screen." This comment was made by Willis P.

I turned to him and was glad to see his cheerful grin. I didn't see him nearly as much as I would have liked. Willis was a Family Circle resident who was a constant flight risk. He was constantly concocting new and ingenious (as ingenious as his level of dementia allowed) ways of escape.

It suddenly occurred to me that I was looking at Willis, even though we were not in the Family Circle. "Willis, how did you get out of the Circle?"

"I just opened the door."

I walked to the door leading to the Family Circle and turned the knob. To my chagrin the knob turned, and the door opened. I lifted my walkie-talkie and conveyed the unfortunate news to the rest of the staff.

Whether due to a design flaw or to a safety measure, all the doors to the Family Circle, whose keypads controlled magnetic locks, had released when the power to the building had been cut. All through the morning, our heavily demented residents had been wandering off, and we had been too preoccupied with every other nuance imaginable in the current circumstances to have even noticed. A headcount of the Circle was taken, and ten residents were missing. They were the ones who, on every other day of the year, continually tried to turn the knobs and push the doors open. This had been their lucky day when the impossible seemed to have happened. The door in fact opened.

Five of the residents were quickly found in the activity room. Two were found sleeping in the beds of other residents, one was found under the desk in Paul's office, and another was found making snow angels in the courtyard. This left one unaccounted for. Opal C. Opal was a sprinter and completely noncommunicative, two things that did not lend themselves toward a happy resolution of her current unknown whereabouts. We carried out another search of the premises, but no trace of Opal was found.

Then, there was a glimmer of hope. Over the radio came Greg's voice, "I've got footprints."

A few minutes later, Paul and Shana met Greg outside one of the exterior exits to the Family Circle. One that was for emergency use only, and, as far as I knew, had never actually been used. Until now. They looked down at the faint outline of fresh footprints leading from the doorway into a nearby ditch.

I had wanted to go with them to continue to search for Opal, but I was told to stay and man one of the other Family Circle entrances and stop anyone else from leaving. Someone had suggested that we block the doors with chairs, but this was quickly overruled as being illegal, and a staff member was assigned to stand next to each of the exits.

"We've got to call the police," Greg said when he was met by Paul and Shana.

"And tell them what?" asked Paul. "That we can't look after our residents?"

"What other choice do we have? She could die out here."

"We could follow her trail," Shana said.

"What are you, a tracker?" Greg asked.

"How hard could it be? We just follow her tracks."

"If you want to go running off into the forest in subzero temperature, following indentations in the snow that may or may not be footsteps, then be my guest. We don't know how long she's been gone for. We need to call the professionals."

"I'm going after her," Paul said.

"Are you crazy? The best thing for Opal is for the police to get involved."

"If we call the police, I'm screwed. I'll lose my job."

"If we don't call the police and they find her it'll look like we didn't even know we had a missing resident."

Meanwhile, inside the Family Circle, I was locked in a circular mind game with Henrietta and Frances and their posse of dementia residents, who were demanding that I step aside and let them through the door, on the other side of which they were convinced was the beach.

"There's a shark warning. I can't let you out," I said.

"We're not going into the water. I promise."

"I trust you. Really, I do. But I'm not allowed to let you out until I get the all-clear from the coast guard."

"I demand you let us out this instant. We've only got a few more hours of good tanning weather."

"Henrietta, you're killing me here."

"You're forgetting who's working for whom."

"Excuse me, sir, Marge needs your help," Vern S said to me. Vern and his wife, Marge, both lived in the Circle, and they were blessed to each have dementia that had progressed at the same rate, so that neither was aware of the other's decline."

"What's wrong, Vern?" I asked.

"Please come with me, she needs help."

"Who?"

"Marge. She needs your help."

"I can't step away from the door. Is she hurt?"

"No, but she's in a rather precarious position."

I lifted my walkie-talkie. "This is Kevin. I need someone to take my post." There was no response. "Hello?" I turned to Henrietta and her entourage. "Wait here," I said. "I'm going to get my swim trunks, and we'll go to the beach together."

"Really? You promise?"

"Yes. But you have to wait for me. I won't get my commission if I'm not with you during your entire stay at the resort."

"We'll be right here."

A few moments later, I followed Vern through his apartment, into the restroom, where Marge was seated on the toilet with her pants and underwear down around her ankles. Vern and I stood at the doorway.

"Hi, Marge. Did you need some help getting up?" Very little outside light was able to filter its way into the corner of the room where Marge was seated, and her face was mostly hidden in darkness.

She nodded.

I walked toward her and began to place my arms beneath her armpits. "Alright, I'm going to count to three, and then up we go." I turned to Vern. "Hey, Vern, I just need you to step back a little and give me some space in case I swing wide."

"I need to be wiped first," Marge said.

"Pardon me?"

My walkie-talkie crackled. "Paul, please come to the reception desk," a voice said over the walkie-talkie.

"I'm unavailable," Paul's voice said.

"It's regarding Opal. The police are here," came the response over the walkie-talkie.

"You need to wipe me first," Marge said to me. "I can't reach."

My attention shifted back to Marge. "What was that?" I asked.

"You need to wipe my bottom first."

"Oh, wow. Um. I'll be right back," I said to her.

In the hallway outside their room door, I withdrew my walkie-talkie. "Attention, Terry. Attention, Terry." Terry was the care staff manager, and the person who I decided should be wiping bottoms when no care staff could be located.

"Greg here, go ahead."

"I'm looking for Terry," I said.

"Sorry."

"Attention, Terry." *Crap.* "Terry come in." *I've got a brown alert situation.* "Has anyone seen Terry?" *I need to be rescued. PLEASE!!!* I wondered what Henrietta and her group were doing. Had they ventured through the door without me? Also, what were the police going to tell Paul about Opal?

Back in the restroom with Vern and Marge I pulled a pair of latex gloves over my hands. *I'm a professional. I can do this.* Remembering Angie's tale from years earlier about how the smell can sometimes penetrate the glove, I put on a second pair.

I crouched next to Marge and wadded up a thick pad of toilet paper.

"First time wiping an old lady's bottom?" she asked.

"Are you kidding me? I do this all the time."

Afterward, in the staff bathroom, I scrubbed my hands furiously. I wished I had had latex protection for my eyes and brain, as well. I was glad, however, that I had been able to help. I was glad, also, that that was not my full-time job.

After drying my hands, my radio crackled. "Terry here."

I walked back to my post in front of the unlocked door and was not surprised to see that Henrietta and her crew were no longer there. Had they forgotten and moved on to something else, or had they attempted to reach the mythical beach on their own? I opened the door and looked out. Paul was standing with two police officers in front of the reception desk. His face was red, and he looked distraught.

"As soon as we finished our search of the property we were going to call," he said.

"And when would that have been? How long after that poor woman had been out in the cold?"

"We were following procedure."

"Clearly, that wasn't good enough."

"No call was made," the other officer said. "So, to us, it looks like you didn't even know she was missing."

"Or that you were just trying to cover your ass."

Paul looked over at me. I closed the door and resumed my post. Standing in front of me now was Frank M. He stood with his hands pressed on his walker staring at the wall. Frank was a former middleweight boxing champion and had a face like a balled-up fist. His eyes were so small and deeply recessed into his head that it looked as though someone had taken the buttons from a child's doll and tried to push them in through his face and tack them to his brain. He smacked his lips together, his toothless gums moving about, trying to form words, though I had no idea which words.

I later learned that one of the police officers had telephoned Paul's boss at the head office and told her of Paul's delay in calling the authorities regarding Opal's disappearance. This was the catalyst that eventually led to Paul's dismissal.

The officers had found Opal walking up a freeway on-ramp, about a mile and a half from Gleeful Meadows. It had become immediately clear to them that she suffered from severe dementia. When they had searched her for identification, they had found a clock radio, a rotary telephone, two remote controls, a hair dryer, four photo frames, and a tea kettle all stuffed down her pants.

Since there were only two assisted living facilities in the immediate area, they didn't have too hard a time figuring out where she belonged. They first took her to Sunny Horizons, our competitor. Upon arrival, they knew she couldn't have been from Sunny Horizons. The officers were met by residents and staff banging on the doors from the inside of the facility. Unlike Gleeful Meadows, Sunny Horizons had sprung for automatic doors. However, since they had such a high turnover of staff, none of their current employees knew how to use the manual overrides for the doors, and everyone had been stuck inside, unable to move between floors or wings. After radioing the fire department to show up with the Jaws of Life, the officers had made their way over to us.

As dinner approached, I was relieved from door duty to help out in the kitchen. Darkness and the cold were rapidly approaching, and we had to work fast to stay ahead of them. A few of the residents' family members, who had the means to do so, had arrived to help out with meals. Furthermore, I was off the hook for activities, as the members of a nearby Church of Latter-Day Saints had arrived with a crate of board games.

We had greater care staff night coverage than we had for the day, as Paul had spent the previous two hours driving through the snow in his SUV, picking up staff members who had been unable to drive in to work on their own.

"What's going on here?" Leona said as she came into the activity room.

"Playing board games," I said.

"Who are all these extra people?"

"LDS."

"You mean Mormons?"

"That's right."

"Well get 'em out of here."

"Why?"

"They're only here to spread their mumbo-jumbo."

"That's not a very nice thing to say. They're only here to play some games. And to cheer you all up."

"That's how they get you. That's how they get in the door. We won't have anything to do with it. Come on, Lloyd."

I watched as Leona and Lloyd left the building and walked along the snow-covered path that ran along the back of the building. As usual,

Lloyd trailed several yards behind Leona. They passed one of our newest care staff, a wonderfully friendly man named Ralph (probably not his birth name), who had recently moved from Kenya. They stopped to speak with him, during which time they shook his hand, and Leona hugged him. After their brief conversation, Ralph continued along the path, while Leona reached down and pulled up a handful of snow. She formed it into a snowball and then called out to Ralph, who turned just in time to catch the snowball right in the face.

I later asked Leona about the exchange with Ralph, worried that, perhaps, there was a racial component to the reason she pelted a snowball at him. Instead, Leona said that Ralph had told her that this was the first time in his life he had ever seen snow. She told him that, the next day, they would build a snowman together and, perhaps, even get into a snowball fight. Ralph said he had seen a snowman once on a Christmas card but didn't know what a snowball fight was. Leona said she'd look forward to showing him. They parted. She formed her snowball, called out his name, and then yelled, "Welcome to America," as she let the ball fly.

After the Mormons had left and everyone had been fed, entertained, and then put down to bed, I finally left for the day. The day had been long, tiring, and a challenge to my sanity. But, then again, didn't that sum up my year of employment in assisted living?

The drive home was slower than that in to work that morning. Those of us in cars that could actually move had to navigate around those that had spun out or run out of gas. I myself ran out of gas, but I had planned ahead and taken a half-full jerry can from the maintenance shed at work, which got me all the way back to my lovely pregnant wife.

I picked up Angie from her work and we slowly and carefully drove the 120 or so miles up to Vancouver to see our families for the weekend. I had come to hate these trips north. It wasn't the drive, but the rush of activity that occurred during these visits. Because Angie usually only ever had one day off at a time, we had to cram all of our visits with family and friends into a twenty-four-hour window. My having divorced parents meant that the bare minimum of obligatory get-togethers was a third greater than it otherwise would be.

Our purpose for this trip was to spend Chinese New Year with Angie's family. This was a doubly important event, as her grandmother was born on Chinese New Year, and therefore it was a birthday celebration as well. I had come to love Angie's family much the same way I love my own. However, there were cultural and family quirks that I suspected would make it impossible for me to ever feel entirely at ease among them. Their bounds on conversational acceptability were much more liberal than the average Westerner. Being called fat to my face had become commonplace. Once, following a period of significant weight gain, I had been called Supersized Kevin. When I first met Angie's mom, she had asked Angie, in Cantonese so as not to offend (ha ha), "Why is he so short?" My nickname among her family is gwai dsai which means white boy.

Although, of course, like any group, they saw only the flaws of others and not their own. "One of the differences between Westerners and Easterners is that we would never put our parents away in old age homes," Angie's uncle said to me. "Westerners don't have the same respect for their elders that we have."

I didn't want to argue with him. I didn't want to say to him that respect of elders ebbs and flows, in all cultures alike, from person to person. That his argument was in league with others that make sweeping generalizations about a particular group. I knew as many Easterners as I did Westerners who had little or no respect for older generations. With regard to his illuminating the greater prevalence in Western culture to seek outside help to assist with the daily care of our geriatric population, did this also illuminate the feelings of shame that the Eastern geriatric population may have toward having their bums wiped by their own children or their grandchildren? Or did their feelings not matter?

I didn't want to tell him that he was speaking from a naiveté that had not experienced what horrors that far side of health had to offer.

Sunday morning, I called Paul to find out how Gleeful Meadows was coping with the storm. "We evacuated," was his answer.

"What do you mean you evacuated?"

"I mean we evacuated the community."

"Gleeful Meadows?"

"Yes, Gleeful Meadows."

"Everybody?"

"Everybody. Right down to Elsie's pet parakeet. We called up every other assisted living facility within a twenty-mile radius that still had power to see if any could take our residents. Amazingly, we found somewhere for every last one of them. We spent all day yesterday loading them onto busses and their beds onto rented trucks."

"You shipped their beds?"

"What else would they sleep on? Fifteen residents went to Dewy Acres alone. They were full to capacity, so the beds were laid next to one another in their lobby."

"That's remarkable," I said.

"More remarkable than that was that, during the whole fiasco, we didn't have a single resident slip into the great beyond."

"The season's young."

"But, even more remarkable, was that an hour after the last bus had left our property the power came back on. All that work for nothing."

"How could you have known?"

"There was a report about it on the local news. But how could we have watched it if the power was out?"

"So are the residents all back?"

"Not yet. We're waiting until tomorrow so we can be staffed up."

"Assuming that there isn't a second storm."

"All the entertainment you booked for the weekend were no-shows."

"Probably dealing with their own set of problems."

"Oh, but the carolers you scheduled actually showed up. They sang to the residents in the blacked-out foyer as we marched them past toward the busses."

"Kind of like the band playing as the Titanic went down."

Most of Monday was spent cleaning the rooms and hallways throughout Gleeful Meadows. The rush to remove beds that hadn't been moved since the building was built had unleashed an extraordinary amount of dust and cobwebs that had danced unrestricted throughout the empty building. There were a couple of brown deposits in toilets within the Family Circle that had been deposited right before the evacuation and whose smells now permeated the air ducts throughout the building.

Bed alarms (which were used to alert staff when residents who needed assistance to stand tried to get out of bed on their own during the night) were now ringing throughout the building. They had been disconnected from the beds but not from the wall outlets. Also, one by one, the oxygen alarms on resident's oxygen compressors began to go off, and we had to follow the sounds throughout the building in order to switch each of them off.

Another problem we had to contend with was the storm, which was still raging. The temperature had risen, and the snow and ice had been replaced with rain and the potential of flood. Our maintenance crew sandbagged the perimeter of the building and placed portable pumps in strategic locations, but it was like placing a Band-Aid over the stump of a severed limb. The water rolled under doors and into the foundation of the building. There were reports from care staff in various areas on the first floor of puddles and ponds forming in residents' rooms. Then, a water pipe that had frozen and ruptured the day before, let go with a torrent through the ceiling of Andy G's room, bringing down ceiling panels and destroying all his property. There was a flicker in the power, and just for a moment, the pumps simultaneously went silent, reminding us of how we would fare that evening without the blessing of electricity.

As Paul considered the prudence of bringing our residents back to Gleeful Meadows, the busses carrying them began to file into our parking lot. It was pandemonium as we moved from bus to bus informing residents of the flooding, while at the same time performing a head count and trying to decide who would be bunking with whom and for how long and what we would do should the power go out again or the flooding get worse or we were hit by an outbreak of the bubonic plague or fell victim to the sadistic whims of a maniac killer or Adeline decided to call the ombudsman and complain about the outdated window treatments in the dining room.

"Get me off this bus," Ariel shouted.

"Please just hold on," I said as I wrote down names as quickly as I could.

"I've been holding it the entire trip. My bowels aren't built for this kind of punishment."

It was then that Frances stood and punched me in the chest. "You fucking motherfucker," she said to me.

I smiled. Everything was back to the way it should be. I was glad that these, my people, my friends, were back, and that our life together could resume. At Gleeful Meadows there was the ever-present feeling of being aboard a sinking ship, but that feeling was never a frightening one as, no matter how crazy our circumstances seemed, there was always mirth amongst us.

Toward the back of the bus, Leona stood and began a chant of, "We're glad to be home. We're glad to be home." As the residents filed off the bus, they all continued the cheer.

"Thank you all so much for everything you do," Iris's daughter said as she brought her mom back into the building. "Having her home with me was a nightmare. I couldn't sleep. I was constantly afraid that she would walk out in the middle of the night or fall down the stairs or drink drain cleaner from beneath the sink. I didn't know or appreciate how hard it was to look after her all day long. And the same stories, over and over. I was ready to kill her."

The only casualty of the storm was Millicent L. At the assisted living community where she and several other residents had spent the day during the power outage, the executive director and marketing director had tried to solicit our residents, offering to undercut the rent and care fees that they paid with us. Millicent was the only resident who didn't tell them to stick their brochure where the sun doesn't shine. When she returned to Gleeful Meadows, that brochure took up a permanent position next to her bedside.

None of us would mourn her loss when she finally did leave, though, unfortunately for her, it was not the departure she would hope for.

CHAPTER ELEVEN

Family

My workday began with a phone call.

"Good morning," I said as I picked up the receiver.

"Help. I need the police," shouted an unfamiliar woman.

"What's wrong?" I could tell from our phone system that the call was originating from the nurse's station in the Family Circle, though I did not recognize the voice.

"Is this the operator?" she asked.

"Yes, it is," I said.

"Quick, please connect me with the police, I've been kidnapped. I don't know where I am."

"Oh, my goodness, I'll get the police for you. Hold while I transfer the call." I paused for a moment. "Police Department, Officer Donner speaking," I said with a stern tone.

"Liar! This isn't the police. It's the same operator who answered before."

I held the phone from my face, unsure of what to say. A moment later I hung up.

"Who was that?" Jennifer asked as she returned from the ladies' room.

"I'm not sure. Did we get a new resident in the Circle last night?"

She checked the logs, and the answer was yes, a woman named Maureen N. Apparently, one of our sister communities had taken in a resident for two weeks while her husband, who took care of her, was out of the country on business. Their intake assessment didn't delve much deeper than her liking of chrysanthemum tea before bedtime. During Maureen's first night at that community, she had awoken in the middle of the night and was convinced she had been kidnapped. She cut the screen of her window and "ran for freedom" in nothing but her nightgown. Her absence was discovered only when she jumped out from behind a bush at a night-shift care staffer, who was out for a cancer stick stroll.

With luck and chrysanthemum tea, they were able to get Maureen back inside and calm her down. The next day, it was decided that she'd complete her temporary stay at our facility because of our supposedly secure Family Circle.

The phone rang again, and I picked it up out of habit.

"Help, I've been kidnapped," the voice said.

I hung up the phone and looked up at a man with a long, gray ponytail holding onto the back of Millicent's wheelchair.

"Can I help you?" I asked with a smile.

"This woman was lying in the bushes along the side of the building with her wheelchair turned over next to her."

"Oh my," I said. "Millicent, what happened?"

"It was horrible. It was just horrible. I was trying to propel myself." She looked up at the man behind her. "I've only got one good arm and one good leg, you know. And they took my motorized scooter away from me. Anyway, I was trying to get some exercise and fresh air, but the sidewalk was so uneven that I lost my balance and toppled over. I thought I was going to die and that no one would find me until after the spring thaw. I'm so fortunate that this young man came along when he did."

The man extended his hand to me. I took it and shook it. "Lance T, senior care auditor for the state," he said.

Over the course of the next hour, we listened to the sound of raised voices emanating from Paul's office and working their way through the ventilation ducts. Through the gossip chain, I learned that we were under the eye and ire of the state, once again for the questionable judgment of one of our weekend care staff. The son of one of our Family Circle residents smelled poop while he was visiting his dad. He had called out for a staff member to come and change his father. The father's usual caregiver was on lunch break, so another began to undress the old fellow. When he removed the man's dirty diaper, he found another dirty diaper, and under that one was a third dirty diaper.

Following her lunch break, the negligent staffer had attempted to defend her actions by insisting that the old fellow had refused to take his soiled diaper off and had, instead, given her permission to place a fresh one over it. She refused to admit that she had done anything wrong.

The last time the state had come for a visit was because a staff member had tried to save time by bathing residents two at a time, and, before that, because a family member had wondered why his mother was limping and found that her toenails had not been trimmed in so long that they had curled under her feet.

The family members of the residents involved in these three incidents of neglect were surprisingly understanding, and each were satisfied when the offending staff member was terminated from their position. However, it was still a requirement for Shana to contact the state regarding the incidents, and the responding investigator was not so magnanimous.

"How could you not be responsible for the care given by your employees?" the state investigator yelled. "Each of your employees is an extension of your own commitment to these residents."

I walked through the hallway of the Family Circle in search of Moira M. She had been moved to the Circle because of her tendency to sleepwalk down the streets of the town. She didn't have dementia, and therefore was out of place amongst the other residents in the Circle. Every day, I would fetch her to participate in activities with the residents in our regular community.

"Hey, you," a woman's voice said behind me.

I turned to see a pale, thin woman in a nightgown, whom I had never seen before.

"Oh, I'm sorry Dr. Green," she said. "I didn't recognize you from the back."

I assumed that this was our new resident. "Good morning, Maureen. It's nice to see that you're adjusting to your new surroundings," I said.

"Adjusting? Oh, Dr. Green, you've got to help me. I'm so glad you're here."

"What's wrong?" I asked.

"These people are holding me here against my will. I need to get out. I don't know if Harry knows where I am."

"Everything is just fine. Everyone here is just trying to help."

"How do you know that? They've asked me to take strange medications. I'm not sure what they want from me."

"I just spoke with Harry and he'll be here in a few days to get you. In the meantime, I'll inquire as to whether the accommodations could be made more to your liking."

After I disengaged myself from Maureen, I found Moira, and the two of us made our way back to the activity room. During the walk, she told me about her sister who had slipped on a piece of dog poo on a sidewalk and had broken her skull and died. "Not picking up your canine's feces is one of the worst crimes a person can commit in our modern society," she had said.

As Moira and I entered the activity room, I saw Hazel's son, Dave, all sun-burned, six foot six inches and 485 pounds of pain in the ass, coming toward me. He was one of those people who was so morbidly out of shape that I wondered how he could have possibly been the best swimmer of his father's sperm. What kind of person would the runner-up sperm have produced if this guy had stopped to check out the scenery or take a nap?

"Hey, Dave," I said.

"I got a bone to pick with you," he said as he thrust his finger at a mote of dust in the air between us.

"What's wrong?"

"We're paying a lot of money for this place, so I'm not a big fan of the fact that my mom has to spend most of the day sitting in her room."

"What do you mean?"

"She told me how nobody comes to get her for meals or activities and that she doesn't get fed unless she ventures out of her room to ask for food."

"I promise you, Dave, your mom's getting three squares a day."

"That's not what she tells me."

Since I was usually hanging out with people's moms and dads as activities director, I tended to be a lot more visible than other directors at Gleeful Meadows—namely those whom these type of concerns should be directed toward—and easier to locate, as my whereabouts were posted on the activity calendar, making it very hard for me to avoid being found.

I never enjoyed dealing with Dave. Most of the family members of residents whom I did interact with, like the majority of society, were kind, decent people. But then there were the assholes, like Dave, who made the enjoyment of everyday living for the rest of us an uncertainty whenever we had cause to interact with them. Dave's position as an asshole, like that of all assholes, precluded him from seeing anyone else's point of view and filled him with the assumption that his position on any given subject was both righteous and uncontestable. He also happened to be someone who refused to admit to himself, or the world, that, as a result of his mother's Alzheimer's, her account of her daily activities and eating schedule here at Gleeful Meadows might not be entirely reliable.

A few months earlier, Shana threatened to have Dave removed from the property by the police and then have a restraining order placed on him, to keep him from setting a single gigantic foot in Gleeful Meadows. The issue that had thrown Dave into a rage that time, during which he told Shana that he'd like to throw her through a window, began with his mom's nocturnal incontinence and her refusal to wear an adult diaper to sleep. Like with Elsie's situation, Hazel's pee dripped from the bed and soaked into the carpet below her. There were only so many times that the carpet could be power washed before it eventually needed to be replaced. After the second replacement, and the lead up to the third, Shana had contacted Dave and told him that Gleeful Meadows was not going to continue to pay for carpet replacement and that it was Dave's turn to foot the bill. That had seemed reasonable to me, although it had not to Dave.

After much swearing, arm waving, ranting and raving (which, perhaps, is just a redundancy for the swearing and arm waving), threats of defenestration and police intervention, Dave agreed to pay for a compromise solution. He would put his money down for linoleum flooring to be rolled out underneath his mom's bed. This way, the cleanup of her pee and stink would be a snap, there'd be no need for further replacement, and when his mom either moved out or died, Dave could roll the linoleum back up and take it away with him for either bathroom or kitchen flooring at home.

Back to the current Dave dilemma: Did I challenge his mother's account to him and remind him of her Alzheimer's disease? Or did I tell him that I'd make sure she was reminded more frequently for meals and activities?

What would you have done?

I was freed from my conversation with Dave by his very own mom, Hazel, who yelled over at me, "Hey, activities boy. Bingo's not going to call itself."

During our third game, Elsie called out, "Bingo," after I had only announced one number. Due to her diminishing hearing, she had not heard me tell everyone to clear their boards and thought that we were still on the previous game. As Elsie called out her numbers, some of which I had not actually called, Adeline began a protest, which was silenced quickly by a slap on the arm from Iris. I happily presented Elsie with her prize as my coconspirators watched.

We learned later that day that the state investigator found that Gleeful Meadows was not at fault for the action of its staff member responsible for the three-diaper incident. However, fault or not, everything gets recorded somewhere, and that record will exist forever, or at least until long after the building is dust, and long after we've all stopped breathing, and therefore caring, whether or not we received citations from state investigators.

As he was leaving, the investigator came up to me in the activities room. "Excuse me?" he said.

I turned to face him. "Can I help you with something?" I asked.

"I saw your name on your nametag. You're the one who reported the financial abuse of Cora by her granddaughter a while back, aren't you?"

"That's right."

He looked around the room and then leaned toward me. "You did the right thing."

He walked away without saying another word.

I spent the rest of the day wondering what more there was in the case of Cora that the state investigator could not tell me. Doing the right thing didn't guarantee a happy outcome. Had my intercession made a difference or had it been too late? I had held within me a sense of dread that I had interfered in affairs that didn't concern me and that I may have irreparably harmed the dynamic within Cora's clan.

My greatest character flaw is that I have a near inability to intentionally be the cause of disharmony between myself and others, or others and others. The vague pronouncement of having done the right thing did not negate the possibility that having done nothing may have been better for their family. However, the devil's advocate within all of us would then say that my interference similarly could just have easily facilitated a *better* outcome for Cora's clan. I will never know.

The most troubling variable within the whole messy affair was the discord that was so evident within the family. How could a granddaughter knowingly and actively seek to defraud her own grandmother? I know that these types of things must happen all the time, but to be within arms' reach of those for whom this was a reality, made real for me our capacity for evil. I was reminded of a story my wife told me of the family of a dying patient of hers who got in a fistfight over the will in the hospital room as their father lay there dying. I only hoped he was not lucid enough for that to have been his final experience on Earth.

Sadly, the Cora situation was not the only instance of horrible-familydom that I witnessed while working at Gleeful Meadows. I'd like to think that life stresses were responsible for such familial discord and that these men and women with whom I had become so close hadn't been enduring these unendurable situations for a lifetime. But, then again, I was seeing only a biopsy of their own attitudes and deeds, not knowing anything at all about what they themselves were like before they became wholly dependent upon those around them.

Leona and Lloyd P left our care after their son and daughter-in-law convinced them that they would be better off moving back to the family farm so that they could look after them themselves. This would have been a beautiful sentiment had the son not first had Leona sign over control of every last penny that she and Lloyd had saved during their long lives to himself. I saw the entire act take place in the corner of the activity room in a beautiful setting next to the fireplace, the son pointing to the dotted line on which Leona signed away her and Lloyd's happiness.

I reported what had taken place, but there was nothing that could be done, as Leona was, as far as anyone knew, of sound mind, and therefore perfectly free to allow herself and her husband to be taken advantage of by their one and only beloved spawn.

At the reception desk, there was a list of names next to the phone of residents' family members who were not permitted to speak to their kin who lived on our premises.

Chastity K's daughter was addicted to crack and hit up her mom for cash every chance she got. Mona M's son was after her to change her will one final time before she died, no doubt favoring him. George M's brother had tried on several occasions to take a two-foot-tall wooden carving from George's room that he claimed George had once stolen from him. Abby C's son-in-law wanted to take advantage of Abby's dementia to get her to divulge the secret recipe for her chocolate almond cake. Norman G's prodigal daughter wanted to move him to a less expensive care facility so there would be more inheritance to receive when he died.

This was just a sampling of the first few names down the list, a list which grew longer each time a new specter of darkness found its way into our midst. Fiends and jackals stalked the perimeter of the property with relentless determination and attempted to sneak in through the phone lines and past the defenses of poorly trained, half-asleep sentries. God help us all.

"What is wrong with you people?" a woman shouted at Jennifer. "My father's only been in the hospital for a day, and you've already cleared out his room."

Paul came out of his office behind Jennifer. "Can I help with something?" he asked the woman.

"I came to get some of my father's belongings, and they've already been cleared out so you can move the next person in. It's a disgrace."

"Who's your father?" Paul asked.

"Richard D, room 206," she said.

"Richard D's room is 406," Paul said. "You'd have known that if you'd shown any concern for him when the reading of the will wasn't so near at hand."

Angie accompanied me to work on the Saturday afternoon that we held a carwash to raise money for the Alzheimer's Association. We were supposed to have been assisted by our local fire department, but a house fire across town took them away from the free hotdogs and poorly painted signs that advertised our washing services.

Our first three customers were all residents of Gleeful Meadows, none of whom owned a car. We received twenty dollars from Adeline for cleaning her walker, ten dollars from Elsie for polishing the spokes of her wheelchair and scraping a piece of gum from one of her wheels, and three dollars and eighty-four cents from Ariel for putting new tennis balls on the back two legs of his walker. I had eaten three hotdogs, and it wasn't even ten thirty in the morning. Angie had come, not only to help wash cars and eat hotdogs, but to help redo the signs that had initially been done the day before.

Nicole had thought it would be a good activity to have some of the residents make the signs. She had drawn the first few to give them templates to follow. When she came back an hour later, after starting concurrent activities with other residents, she found that the signs that had been produced by her residents were both illegible and incomprehensible. I had had a similar experience before Christmas when I had asked Tom to help me write "Happy Holidays from Gleeful Meadows" on cards that were sent out to the families. I had been summoned to Paul's office a few days later and asked why he was receiving calls from angry family members regarding cards they had received from us that read, "Happy Hairball from Gary Marry" or "Holy Happy from Hippy Marshmallows."

The next person in line for a free hotdog was Georgina M, the daughter of Virginia M. Virginia was dying from lung cancer and whom, each morning, we thought would never wake up. "One dog, please," she said.

Virginia removed her oxygen mask. "Make that two, will ya, Kevin?"

Georgina turned to her mom, "You're not supposed to have this kind of food. You've got to watch your salt intake."

"But..." Virginia tried to say.

"Just one," Georgina said to me.

As she handed me an empty bun, Angie gave me a look that said, *What a bitch. How can she deny her dying mother the satisfaction of a hotdog? If that was my daughter, I would strangle her with my breathing hose.* The look I gave Angie as I placed a hotdog into the awaiting bun said, *I know. I see this kind of crap all day long and it makes me sick.*

Next in line for a free dog was Paul. I handed him his plate as he looked triumphantly at the turnout, which had been growing steadily all morning. Of the residents holding placards advertising the carwash, two were holding them with the signage facing us instead of the street, and one had nothing on his sign at all.

"How much longer until the little one arrives?" he asked Angie.

"About two months. Give or take."

"Then your fella here is going to become Mister Mom?" He gestured to me.

I had decided conclusively that I would stay at home full-time with our son and had told the residents and given Paul my notice on the same day. Paul had expected the decision, and the conversation with him was more of a formality than anything else. The residents, on the other hand, were a completely different story. For many of them, it was as though a jolt of electricity had been administered. This is not necessarily because of their attachment to me specifically, but rather their attachment to whomever held the role as activities director. You were their full-time best friend, and, by leaving, it was like you were severing the friendship.

"You're leaving us?" Marcia had asked for the fifth time that day. "You can't leave us. It's not fair."

"He's not really going to leave," Cora said. "He's going to bring that precious little baby in with him every day, and we're going to help him look after it."

"I think it's wonderful what you're doing," Lucille S said. "I always felt bad for the men of our generation, because they weren't allowed to make the decision to stay at home with their little ones. Society made them go out and be the breadwinners and, therefore, imposed a distance between them and their children that didn't exist between the children and their moms."

"It's not right for the man to be home," Grace said. "He needs to be making the living."

"You're leaving us?" Marcia asked again. "You can't leave us. It's not fair." Until my very last day at Gleeful Meadows, Marcia would continually forget and then subsequently find out repeatedly for the first time that I had decided to leave and would again be broken-hearted.

As an aside, upon my first visit back to Gleeful Meadows with my newborn baby, after having left the company, Marcia hadn't even remembered who I was.

"Since you're leaving anyway," Paul said with a mouthful of hotdog, "I guess you won't mind that I'm going to have to cut your budget starting this week."

"Of course, I mind. How come?"

"Because of our occupancy. We're only seventy-five percent full, so I'm cutting back your budget by twenty-five percent."

"That doesn't make any sense," I said.

"Every other director has cut back. You're the only one who hasn't."

"It's easy for Eric to cut back, because he only needs to feed the number of people who live here. Shana only needs the medical supplies for the residents we have, Greg's staff only need to clean occupied rooms, and Terry only needs seventy-five percent caregiver coverage. But what am I supposed to do, only put gas enough in the bus to drive *most* of the way to our outings? Give out even crappier prizes at bingo? And I'm already scraping the bottom of the entertainer barrel. If I pay these people any less to come and perform, we're going to have to get street performers in here to play."

"Hire more volunteers with better skills."

"When people come in for tours of our facility, they see us cutting corners. If the activities suck—"

"If the activities suck, that's your fault. You're paid to be creative."

"Yes, but not to make wine out of water."

"This isn't a negotiation," he said.

"We've got to spend money to make money."

"That's easy to say when it's not coming out of your pocket."

"Well, whose pocket is it coming out of? Certainly not the owner's."

"Careful there."

"All I'm saying is that the image of this place is based as much on the activities as it is on clever advertising. The advertising gets people in here, but the smiles on residents' faces as they partake in engaging activities is what sells rooms."

A short time after my conversation with Paul, I was approached by Ida, whose mother Bernice I had dubbed the Blue Hare. "Paul's a real bummer," she said.

"Yeah, he's always had a stick up his butt."

"My mom told me that he stopped you all from singing karaoke in the activity room because he thought it sounded bad having a bunch of old ladies sing Elvis tunes."

"That's the unofficial version."

"Well, if you need any help with things, I'd love to pitch in."

"That'd be great. Any interest in coming to see a musical next month? I'll need some chaperones to help, considering Paul just pulled the care staff out from under me."

"Is my mom going?"

"Are you kidding? She was the first one to sign up."

That night, I sat at the computer and stared at the next month's activities calendar, now mostly empty. I had redone the budget and removed a good portion of the fun. I had decided to think more creatively about where my budget money was placed. The ladies loved stuffed animals for bingo prizes, so, first thing in the morning, I would go to a secondhand thrift store, buy every stuffed animal I could find that didn't look as though it had been sprayed by wayward bodily fluids, and throw them in the wash. I had made a photocopy of the doctor and dentist appointments that were already scheduled for the following month, and, since the gas used for appointment runs didn't come out of my budget, I scheduled various outings to correspond with those appointments.

Another brainchild was that I went through the employee files to see what special skills or hobbies had been listed on their applications. After an hour of research, I had made a list of musicians, martial artists, a juggler, a ventriloquist, a competitive unicyclist, an opera singer, and a horse trainer. What these people were doing working here I hadn't a clue.

After that, I began making calls and was able to find enough of the skilled staffers, who were excited enough to share their ability, to come unpaid on a day they weren't working to entertain our folks.

I filled in the calendar and was pleased to see that I had found enough free labor and other loopholes to offset my reduced budget.

The only other challenge I had to face in the immediate future was the trip to see *Bye Bye Birdie* the following month, that I had scheduled for the first fourteen residents who had signed up for the event. I had arranged with Terry to have two of her staff assigned to me for three hours, to accompany me and the residents to the performance. Paul had now put the kibosh on that.

"I'm screwed," I said out loud to myself.

"What's wrong?" Angie asked.

"I don't know what I'm going to do about the trip to the play. I can't find anyone else who'll go with me, other than Ida."

"I'll go with you."

I turned to look at her. "Are you kidding me? You're bogged down with your own crap."

"I can take a few hours out to go see a play."

I stood and kissed her. "You are so great."

One thought that had eluded me until now was how lucky I was to have the support of my family: Angie. I had seen so many examples of families who were not supportive of each other, and here I had a wonderful wife, who was helping me out in a simple way, yet, for others, it would have come with strings attached or not come at all.

I've been taking notes for a long time about the kind of father I want to be. With a child on the way, it was cram time. Luckily, I had plenty of examples around me of the type of parent I did not want to be. As a child of divorce, and a friend of children from loveless marriages, I was left with the unanswerable question of how things could go so terribly wrong with some families and yet so wonderfully right with others?

"...So, we took him back, and they give us the one with the marks on his head that was my baby," Iris said, finishing up her story.

I looked up as Marty F came into the activity room with his dad. They sat on a sofa in the corner of the room, each with a cup of cocoa in their hand. Marty's face was bruised from an incident that had transpired the previous week, which promised to ensure that his brother, Raymond, wouldn't be coming around Gleeful Meadows in the near future to harass his father. Broke and frustrated, Raymond had gone to Marty's house in an attempt to force him to give up some of their father's savings. Raymond had brought a .38 special, with which he repeatedly pistol whipped Marty into submission. Luckily, one of the neighbors had heard the commotion and called the police. Before the standoff ended, Marty had thought he would die as he looked past the barrel of the pistol at his enraged brother, smelling the alcohol, and knowing that, if he died, his father wouldn't be far behind.

As I watched Marty and James together in the corner of the room, I wondered how such a gentle man could produce such a violent and vindictive offspring as Raymond. But, then, I again remembered that I rarely knew anything about what our residents were like in their personal lives before they came to reside at Gleeful Meadows. Without knowing what kind of father James had been to Raymond, I had no right to cast judgment or opinion on either of them.

We had had a new resident move in earlier that week. Actually, we had had two move in, one of whom had already moved out. The circumstances for the one who had moved out after only two days was that the family had suspected that a staff member had pilfered money from their mom's room. The daughter had given her mother two hundred and fifty dollars in case she wanted to purchase anything during group outings into the community. The problem with this scenario was that the mom was a resident of the Family Circle, and, although theft is always a possibility, she could have just as likely used the money for toilet paper and flushed it down the toilet or simply eaten it. The move-in paperwork specifically stated not to give any money to Family Circle residents, but, repeatedly, family members didn't want to see their loved one in the new light of illness and diminishing mental capacity and, instead, continued to treat them as they did in their previous life. There were other quirks of life in the Family Circle that many families had difficulty accepting. One such quirk was the phenomenon of musical beds that some of the residents engaged in. Family would visit and find their loved one snuggled up under the covers with another resident. This was not a sexual coupling (which also existed in such communities), but, rather, the very human need to be held and comforted.

We had had several rapid move ins/move outs in the past several months, and not all were a result of unrealistic expectations from family members. There were always problems with staff cutting corners, and there were problems with the building, which was old and continually showing its age.

The newest resident whom we were trying desperately to hold onto was Hollace M. Holly (as she preferred to be called) was a sweet lady, whose daughter was such a dreadful human being, that I wondered how Holly had not smothered her as a child. If she had, Holly's own end possibly would not have been so sudden, tragic, and unnecessary.

I was still thinking about the letter we had received from Millicent L's daughter earlier that day, which read:

To the Executive Staff of Gleeful Meadows,

> *The care and well-being of my mother and her assets have been turned over to me following the death of Doreen. I am afraid that I could never be as meticulous in my role of Power of Attorney as Doreen was, and I fear, as a result, would no doubt lead to the inevitable conclusion of her complete depletion of the few remaining savings she has left. I am, therefore, left with no other alternative than to turn her care over to the state.*

> *Thirty days from the writing of this letter, she will be moved to a state-run facility, who will also take over the responsibility of her finances. Thank you for the care you have given my mother thus far. She just requires too much care than either of us is capable of providing.*

> *Sincerely,*
> *Susan K*

As I was entering the activity room, I was approached by Cathy, Hollace M's daughter. "I put a dollar value on your services and deducted it from our monthly bill, as I don't need my mom taking part in your activities."

"Have you run this by Paul?" I asked.

"I'm running it by you. You can run it by Paul if you think that's necessary."

"What's Holly going to do all day?"

"That's up to her, isn't it?"

"So, it was her choice not to take part in the activities?"

"I've also made a doctor's appointment for her this evening, and we're going to need you to drive us. That's not really an activity, so we're still not paying for any."

I started to respond, but Cathy turned around and left. I shrugged my shoulders and joined the circle of ladies who had assembled for morning exercises. A moment later, Cathy came back into the room, pushing her mother in her wheelchair. She wheeled her into the corner of the room and angled her chair so she was facing us in the center.

The woman's wheelchair had four small wheels instead of two small and two large and, therefore, made it impossible for her to use her arms to propel herself anywhere. We all turned and looked at her. Dorothea waved.

"She's just going to sit here and watch," Cathy said. "She's not going to participate." Cathy turned to her mom. "You're not going to participate. I'll be back later in the day to take you to your appointment." She kissed her mom on the cheek and then left.

Throughout the course of our exercises, I couldn't help looking up at the sad-looking woman in the corner of the room. She made no effort to attempt the exercises, no doubt having been told by her daughter not to do so. I didn't know whether I should wheel her into the circle with us or let her be.

"She too good for the rest of us?" Hazel asked.

"She's just shy," I answered.

Somewhere in the room, a cell phone began to ring. I turned to Holly, who was looking all around herself for the source of the ringing. I noticed that she had a cell phone dangling from a string around her neck. She finally found it and answered it. "Hello?" she said. "This is Holly. Cathy, is that you? I'm not doing anything. You told me I couldn't. Just sitting here. I'll wait until you get here. They're all looking at me right now. I don't know why. I'm not doing anything wrong. I'm not. Okay, bye."

Cora's daughter sighed into the phone. "I'm not paying for my mother to go to a play."

"She said she'd like to go," I said.

"She won't even remember that she went. What's the point?"

"The point is that she'll enjoy herself while she's there. She doesn't need to remember it tomorrow. Tomorrow, we'll be doing something else fun that she won't need to remember the next day. Hello? Hello?" She had hung up. I put down the receiver.

I was supposed to have left work early that day due to overtime I had logged the week previous. However, since I was the only bus driver on the property, I had to wait around to retrieve Hollace from the appointment I had driven her and her daughter to earlier in the day.

I sat in my office and stared at the ultrasound photographs of my son. At the appointment, when we had been told it was a boy, we had been shown an image of what was supposedly his penis. The image looked more like it contained a flavored marshmallow from a box of Lucky Charms than it did a phallus.

I wondered what my son would be like. Would he be healthy? Would he be strong? I thought about a conversation I had had earlier in the day when Greg had said he would have been naturally selected to die an early death were it not for modern medicine and technology. Greg had severe sleep apnea and required a breathing machine while he slept, the presence of which kept him from the hypertension, heart arrhythmias, and stroke that are associated with apnea. He also had a lazy eye that was so off center that, without corrective lenses, he could barely walk due to such strong vertigo. I also thought about one of the housekeepers at Gleeful Meadows whose daughter had had open-heart surgery when she was barely a week old. With all the things that could go wrong with the human body, it seemed virtually impossible that any of us could be born in working order. Yet time and again we were. More often than not, the miracle of procreation played out with perfection, so that it all seemed so deceptively simple.

I took solace in the notion that the overwhelming majority of babies had to be born healthy, otherwise we couldn't survive as a species. My baby would be born just fine. And, if he wasn't fine, he would be born the way he was supposed to be born.

Would he be proud of his father? This question tugged away at my soul in a way that made it difficult for me to rationalize into submission. All kids, at some point in their lives, resent their parents. It's all part of growing up and finding our own path in life. But would he resent the fact that I was not a more traditional father? That I was not the breadwinner, like the male archetype our society dictated? Little did I know that this was a question I would likely wrestle with for the rest of my life.

I awoke to the ringing of the phone on my desk. The side of my face was warm and covered in drool. I picked up the receiver. "Hello?"

"Cathy just called," Jennifer said. "It's time to go pick them up."

I looked at my watch. It was past seven o'clock. "It's about time. How many tests do they need to run on the lady?"

I got into the bus and checked the rat trap behind the driver's seat. It was unoccupied, and I wasn't sure if that was a good thing or not. A rat had been getting into the bus through a hole in the back of the glove box. Eric, our chef, had seen it exiting for a morning food run and chased it around the bus with a rake. Lately, the only evidence of its presence were chunks it had eaten out of my city map.

As I drove slowly through the parking lot, I steered wide of Paul and Shana, who were trying to wrangle Maureen N, who had slipped out of the Family Circle, and was now running laps around the parking lot in her nightgown. "Help, fire. Help, fire," she shouted.

It was my third trip to the hospital that day. Earlier, I had come to retrieve Dorothea, who had fallen asleep in her deck chair and tumbled forward onto the pavement in the courtyard. She had insisted she was fine, but living in the era of frivolous litigation, we didn't take a chance.

"I'm going to miss bingo if you send me off," she had said.

"We'll have someone play for you," Shana answered.

"But they don't know my system, and it would take me too long to explain it to you."

"It'll be fine."

"My cards have to both have a ten in the upper left-hand corner and a sixty-two in the lower right. You got that?"

"I think so," Shana said as she looked up at the medics coming through the door with a stretcher.

"And I need to have exactly fifty chips. Forty-eight red and two black for the center square. That one's free you know? Did I mention that I like to play two boards at once? Sometimes, if one's a dud or a loser, I like to change it up for the next game. You got all that?"

After the hospital staff had run their tests and were sure that Dorothea was fine, I had been summoned to retrieve her. I had waited while she showed her doctor her teeth with a big grin. "I'm ninety-four, and I still have all my own teeth. Can you believe it? Not even my kids can say the same. Dentures, all of them."

But that was then, and this was now. As I drove through the darkened parking lot of the outpatient part of the hospital, I slowed at each doorway to read the stenciled numbers above the door. In the distance, I could see the flashing lights of an ambulance.

The rain was heavy, and the flashing red of the ambulance made it hard for me to make out any of the addresses or physician names on the exteriors of the buildings. I stopped the bus outside a door whose address was hidden by a tree, which seemed to be leaning up against the building. I threw the gear shift in park and got out into the rain and approached the door. When I saw that the address was not the one I was searching for, I headed back to the bus.

I repeated this process as I got closer to the ambulance at the end of the parking lot. Soon, there were no offices left, except the one before which the ambulance sat. I got out and walked into the foyer. Hollace was stretched out on the floor while the paramedics attended to her. Cathy stood to the side with a look of disorientation. There was a moment where everyone looked up at me in unison, before the paramedics resumed their work with Hollace.

"This is your fault," Cathy screamed at me.

"What happened?" I asked.

"Step back, please," one of the paramedics said to me.

"If you had come when you were supposed to, this wouldn't have happened," Cathy said.

"What happened?"

"She fell in the bathroom."

"I came as quickly as I could. I'm sorry she fell, but I got here as soon as I could."

"This is your fault."

I was shaking as I drove back to Gleeful Meadows. The accusation that I was somehow responsible for Hollace's injuries made me nauseous. The feeling was reminiscent of when Sarah had informed me of the accusation that I had struck Selma.

The only passenger to ride back with me in the bus that night was Hollace's empty wheelchair. We would learn the next day that she had broken her hip in the fall. I would not see Hollace again, and that image of her on the floor with the paramedics over her was the last image of her that I would be left with. I would also learn that exactly what had happened before I had arrived was that Hollace had told Cathy that she needed to use the restroom. Cathy had told her to wait until they got back to Gleeful Meadows. Hollace eventually told Cathy that she could no longer hold it and needed to use the restroom at the clinic. Cathy told her to go ahead but to be quick. Hollace was no longer physically able to use a toilet without assistance, and, for whatever reason, Hollace did not ask Cathy for that assistance, and Cathy did not offer it.

As I lay awake that night in bed, I wondered to myself whether family was a blessing or a curse. The more you love them, the more you stand to be hurt by them, whether it's through their actions, their injuries, their sorrows, or their deaths. I have seen such wonderful family interactions, both in my personal life and at Gleeful Meadows, yet it is the memories of the shameful ones that stay with me long after the deeds or words that had been cast upon their victims have receded into the past.

"Something on your mind?" Angie asked.

"Not anymore."

"You want to talk about it?"

"Not anymore," I said.

I had been thinking about lots of things, none of which were happy. Most recently my thoughts were of Dave and his inability to accept his mother's physical and mental decline and how he took out his rage and frustration on those around him. I had been thinking of a way to force him to confront her memory loss without calling him or his mom a liar. At dinnertime that day, I had done it, and I hoped it was in a manner that would help both him and Hazel.

Dave had come to the community to have dinner with his mom. I had watched from the periphery of the dining room as they ate in silence. After the meal, they sat for some time, each sipping a cup of coffee. After they had finished their coffee and were about to get up and leave was when I made my move.

"Hi, Dave. Hi, Hazel," I said as I approached their table.

"Evening," they said in unison.

"What are you going to have for dinner tonight, Hazel?" I asked.

"I don't know, but I'm starving."

"But, Mother, you've already eaten," Dave said.

"What do you mean I've already eaten?" I heard Hazel say as I walked away.

CHAPTER TWELVE

Death

A s I was sitting here writing this, an email popped up on my computer screen from a friend and former coworker at Gleeful Meadows informing me that Ariel S had just passed away. I hadn't seen him on my last several visits to the community. He had withdrawn from those around him, even more than was usual for him. Many of the residents I knew and had become close with while working at Gleeful Meadows have died since my leaving. I will not mention them here, as this book was never meant to be a list of the dead, nor the dead meant to be the timekeepers for how long it took me to complete this manuscript. We all die, and if I shelve these pages long enough, everyone within them, and everyone they knew and who loved them and whom they loved, will also die.

When coming to work in the senior care industry, no one prepares you for the sense of personal loss you will feel. They don't prepare you for the mass death rate of close friends. Sure, you see more death working in a hospital, but you don't spend your days gossiping and playing indoor lawn bowling with the patients. There's professional detachment. We're professional in assisted living and nursing homes as well, but how could you not become platonically intimate with those who live there? You fill a void in each other's lives—to care or to be cared for—and it's hard when that fragile bond is severed. Let alone constantly. They become your closest friends, and then die at a rate where you are scarcely coming to terms with the death of one when the death of another comes along soon after.

Now imagine how it is for the residents who live in these communities. Most of their friends have already died (the average age in assisted living and nursing care is higher than the average senior age out in the real world), so they move into a place with contemporaries whom they haven't outlived, only to make new friendships—close ones—only to watch them all die around them.

That season at Gleeful Meadows, before the birth of my son, we had had our fill of death. We had lost friends, and then lost the friends who had helped keep our spirits up through the previous losses. However, the worst was still to come.

If this was a work of fiction, I would build the suspense. Keep you guessing and wondering if the concierge had done it, or whether a tooth found in a bowl of soup, or an offhand remark made to a hack accordion player were, in fact, clues left along the way to keep you turning the pages until the very end. The truth with life is that we are not kept in suspense during the lead up to the striking of tragedy. It comes at us without warning, like a bolt of lightning we are sure was meant for someone else.

The death of our residents, although sad, was not so difficult to come to terms with as they had each already had long and fruitful lives, and they were each playing in overtime innings.

On a lonely night, filled with tears and alcohol, one of our caregivers, pretty, young, and seemingly so full of joy and promise, put a gun to her mouth and blew the back of her head all over her bedroom wall. This would prove to be the final challenge to the morale of our community before my leaving it.

Whenever something like this happens, those who knew the person try to dissect the days and months and years, and the seconds, of life and gestures and speech for significance and meaning that had escaped notice, which could possibly help us explain the why. No syllable or gesture is left unmolested by our attempts to understand and, perhaps, for some self-destructive streak on our own part, to take upon ourselves some blame and guilt for ignoring the cries for help that had been laid out before us.

Mike B, Tom's son, came in through the front doors of the building and walked up to the reception desk. "I'm here to close out my dad's account," he said.

As was now typical, Jennifer was nowhere to be seen, and I had been taking advantage of some down time and was checking my email at her computer. I stood when I saw Mike and reached out to shake his hand. "You're dad's not coming back?" I asked.

"My dad died two nights ago," he said.

"Oh, Mike, I'm so sorry."

"Thanks. Yeah, he was one of a kind, all right."

I hadn't seen Tom since the day he had collapsed during the walk some time ago. We had made several enquiries about his condition and were told each time that he would be coming back when he was stronger.

"I should have known that he wasn't getting any better," Mike said. "I thought if I kept him in the hospital, I would be doing the best by him; it turned out I was doing the exact opposite. This was his home, and I never really understood that. I always thought of this place as nothing but a glorified nursing home, but, the truth is, he loved it here. Right at the end, he was really bad, I mean, I've never seen him like that. Not himself. Not with it, if you know what I mean. He kept sitting up and looking around and asking for Marvin."

"One of his caregivers," I said.

"Yeah. He should have been here at the end. This is where he should have been. I don't think dying would have been so hard for him if he had been in his own room with people around him he knew. I did wrong by him."

I put a hand on Mike's massive shoulder. There was nothing I could say to console him. It wasn't his father's death he was mourning, but the decisions he himself made before the death that now would forever haunt him.

The part of my job I hated the most was being the manager on duty over the weekend, a less-lofty-than-it-sounded position that rotated around to all the directors. I never had any serious emergencies to deal with as the head-fellow on the property. Other directors, with less experience than I, had had to worry about the death of residents, burst sewer pipes, missing residents, mass staff revolt, guinea pig infestation, and dining room food poisoning. I, on the other hand, had been spared from serious disaster and, instead, had to contend with staff trying to take advantage of my nice-guy persona.

The day always began with an inspection of the community for anything that might be out of the ordinary, which, unfortunately, includes conversations with staff members whom I wouldn't encounter on any other day. These judgments were not mine alone. After first meeting Vivian, Angie wondered if she was missing a chromosome or two. After first meeting Liv, Angie thought she was an especially young, heavily demented, resident of the Family Circle. Some of the weekend staff were great, but the dregs of our employment circle had definitely been allocated to the nights and weekends.

I walked up to Helena, one of our care managers at our third-floor nursing station, preparing a resident's medication. She was dressed in pink spandex leggings and a neon blue crop top.

"Good morning, Helena," I said.

"Hey," she said over her shoulder.

"Yeah, well, I'm MOD today, so I'm just doing my morning rounds, checking on things. I was just wondering why you're not wearing your uniform."

"It's Sunday."

"But it's not casual Sunday."

"You heard what happened down in California. I'm just trying to protect myself. You know, as a woman. You wouldn't understand."

Two weeks earlier, someone had called an assisted living community in Palm Springs. They called during the night, knowing that one of the graveyard crew would answer. "You, in the red shirt and tan pants (the uniform that all staff at that facility wore), I'm in the building right now, and I'm coming to kill you."

"What I don't understand is how not wearing a uniform is going to protect you from prank callers. And, by the way, where's Mona? I haven't seen her yet today."

"She's not coming in. Her daughter's sick."

"Her husband doesn't have a job. Can't he take care of their daughter?"

"He's gotta be out looking for work."

"On a Sunday?"

"You gotta be ready to look all the time."

"So, if I called Mona's house right now, she'd answer, because she'd be home looking after her daughter, not at the beach or out shopping?"

When I got back to my office, I saw that the message light on my phone was blinking. I hit the speakerphone button and dialed into the message. "Yeah, it's me, Marcus. I can't come in to work today because I got bit on the leg by a termite. Later, bro." I had never actually met Marcus. He had called in sick every day that I had been MOD. His excuses have included: being hit by a baseball bat, food poisoning, Lyme disease, blood transfusion, and amnesia. I kept waiting for him to up the ante with Ebola or anthrax.

My intercom beeped. "Kevin? Kevin, I need to speak with you." I didn't say anything. "I know you're in there, I can hear you trying to be quiet."

"What is it, Grace?" I said.

"Can you come to my room?"

"Are you asking me on a date?"

"I think our new man is stealing from us."

"I don't want to hear it, Grace."

"You don't care that he's a thief?"

"What did he steal?"

"I don't think I care for your tone," she said.

"What's wrong with my tone?"

"As resident council president, it's my right to have an immediate meeting with the senior staff member on property if there's an issue that I feel needs immediate attention. Senior staff is you, bucko."

"What did he steal?"

"Well, now I'm not going to tell you."

"Have a nice day, Grace."

"Just get over here."

Grace was what a polite person would call "feisty." She had a voice like broken glass sliding across sandpaper from a lifetime of smoking and swore with rampant gaiety. She pulled around an oxygen tank on wheels wherever she went, though instead of pumping air into her lungs, her face mask was usually slung over her shoulder as she claimed this made her less desirable to men. The paradox of Grace was that she had made her living as a classical concert pianist. However, only her name reflected her ability with a piano. The first time I met Grace I said, "So, I hear you play the piano." She responded, "And if you think you're going to get a free performance out of me, you've got another thing coming." Apparently, the last assisted living community she had lived in used her as free entertainment. Every time she sat down to play the piano in their activity room, the care staff would drag all the residents out of their rooms to listen. Unfortunately, Grace was also arrogant about her abilities and, whenever I hired a pianist to perform, she would sit at the back of the room and scoff, snort, and heckle.

"What are these walls made with? Cheesecloth?" Grace said as I came into her room. "I can hear the lady in the room next to me having bowel movements. Bowel movements! Get her some Metamucil or get me some ear plugs." She shook the ash off of a cigarette into her oxygen mask, which she held upturned in her lap.

"Are you trying to kill us all?" Maria, one of our caregivers, asked as she walked toward Grace's tank. "You're going to blow up the whole building."

"Don't have a stroke, dear. I only turn the tank on for special occasions."

"Maria, could I have a word in private with Grace?" I said.

"Well? Get going before I kick you in your A-frame," Grace said to her.

"I thought you had a dress code here for the caregivers. How come I get the girl who looks like she's about to go stand on a street corner? She walks around here in her hussy getup."

I just shook my head at her.

After prying myself loose from Grace and her crazy making, I wandered down the hallway, and I looked in through the glass door of our chapel, where the memorial for Norma B was being held. I was touched by the number of people in the room, both young and old, those who lived at Gleeful Meadows, and family who had traveled from afar. Those gathered laughed as Norma's son told a humorous anecdote about his mother. In the corner of the room, I saw Roy, Norma's husband, who was also a resident at our community. I knew that he wouldn't live much longer without having Norma by his side.

Norma's death had come unexpectedly—or as unexpectedly as can be expected for a woman in her nineties. I wondered how enjoyable her life possibly could have been in her final years. She had become blind and deaf and was confined to a wheelchair and shunned by most of the residents because she sometimes yelled out uncontrollably.

My fondest memory of her was during bingo, when I would wheel her up next to me at the caller's table and place the chips on her board for her. Every once in a while, when I was sure no one would notice, I would even cheat for her. Another memory that ranks a close second was when I had first begun working at Gleeful Meadows and was holding a door open for Norma and the caregiver pushing her wheelchair. I said,

"Good morning, Norma, it's nice to see you." She replied, "It's nice to see you, too, even though I can't see a damn thing."

I hadn't been there when she had died, but had arrived at work as they were bringing the stretcher with her body on it out of the building. I knew that, one day, I wouldn't even remember her name.

My next run-in that day was with Cheik, another of our caregivers. "Where you been, man?" he said when we nearly ran into each other in a stairwell. Cheik had his jacket on, and I knew this conversation was going to be a bad one.

"What's with the jacket, Cheik? It's like a thousand degrees in here."

"I gotta go, man," he said.

"You're not feeling well?" I asked.

"I feel fine, I just gotta go."

"You've got to work is what you gotta do. You've got people to look after. Sick, elderly people. Have you given out the noon meds yet?"

"I'm tired of taking orders."

"So am I, but it's called having a job."

"I'll see you around."

"What do you mean you'll see me around? You can't walk off the job and then decide to come back, you know."

"What do I care? I'll have another job when I want one."

This was a scam I had quickly become aware of after I had moved into my position of quasi-management. When Cheik had applied for the job of caregiver at Gleeful Meadows, he had supposedly only been in the country for a few weeks. There were already countrymen of his on staff who vouched for him being a standup guy. His country of origin was war-ravaged, which made retrieving any overseas references impossible. After a splendid interview, he began two weeks of training, which would have been followed by several more weeks of light, supervised work. During this time, a background check was processed on the social security number of an entirely different someone else from the same country. Cheik had most likely been in the United States for years, moving from job to job, continually being vouched for by people he either knew directly, or whom he was put in contact with by countrymen in common. Cheik was the first, but unfortunately not the last, person I'd come across using this scam. Sometimes, they decided to come back to work, knowing that we could never outright accuse them of cheating the system. Often they knew that their job would be waiting for them, as we absolutely needed staff to care for our seniors, no matter how unreliable they might be.

This loophole, created by our needing them more than they needed their job, led to numerous situations like the above-mentioned, along with staff members giving one-day notice before taking a vacation, and poor attitude while on shift. They did not fear censure or firing. In another industry, this behavior would seem comical, and might have even brought silent nods of approval from others for these employees' readiness to "stick it to the man." However, in the case of healthcare and senior care, the only people who are ill-affected by this behavior are those whom we are there to care for.

I have worked with many fine people on the other extreme, ones whose work ethic was so righteous and unwavering that you would think that the very fate of their own souls was held in the balance by the care they provided to the seniors in their charge.

One such individual was a caregiver named Megan. She had the type of personality that lifted the spirits of others with whom she came into contact, a personality that was a gift to the residents in the Family Circle with whom she spent her days.

"Why are you always in such a good mood?" I asked as I watched her serve snacks to residents in the Family Circle lounge room.

"Why are you?" she asked of me.

"I asked you first."

"Are you two going to get married or something?" Murray W asked as he began eating his bagel and cream cheese.

"It's refreshing. But it's also unusual," I said.

"I love what I do."

"No one else around here seems to."

"You do."

"So, are we the sane ones or the crazy ones?"

"We're the ones with potential for other things," she said.

"This isn't a lifelong gig for you?"

"Wiping butts? No. Senior care? I'm not sure yet."

"What did you do before this?"

"Army."

"You're kidding."

"Best job I ever had."

"Why'd you leave?"

"To get a little more life experience."

"You'll get an overdose of that here."

"I'd like to go back to school too."

"We're not getting any younger," a voice called out.

"We'll continue this later," I said. Megan and I smiled at each other.

When I entered the activity room to see what my ladies were up to, I saw them gathered around Iris as she concluded: "...So we took him back and they give us the one with the marks on his head that was my baby."

"Where you been all day?" Bernice asked me.

"Working."

"Your job is supposed to be in here with us."

"Not when I'm manager on duty it's not. I've got to throw my weight around."

"You couldn't throw your weight around if you were sitting on a slingshot. And what's with the clipboard?"

"I thought it made me look important."

"That might work on people who don't already know you. Everyone around here already knows you're not important."

"And if I walked around really fast, I thought people would think I'm on my way to take care of something really important."

"We all thought you were just showing off because you *can* walk fast."

Later I sat in my office, thankful that the day had ended (at least the part of it that I was responsible for) without any major catastrophes.

I came in the next morning to the news that Grace had died during the night. My only thought was that I was glad it hadn't happened during the day while I was in charge. No, that's not true. Other thoughts came to me. I remembered the only time I had heard her at the piano. It was late, and I had come back into the activity room for my coat. She wouldn't have continued had she known I was there, so I stood in the darkness and closed my eyes as her music filled me.

There was a note on my office door that Paul wanted to see me. I went to his office and closed the door behind myself.

"What's up?" I asked.

"How long did it take you to get to the clinic?"

"What clinic?"

"Last week. To fetch Hollace and Cathy."

"Why?"

"Cathy is claiming that you took an unreasonable amount of time to pick up her and her mom."

"I can't control the traffic."

"Was the traffic the only delay?"

"I left the building as soon as Jennifer told me Cathy had called. But it doesn't matter, the time it took is irrelevant. She should never have made her mom go to the bathroom on her own. She should have helped her." I didn't mention that, when I had returned to Gleeful Meadows that night, Jennifer had informed me that she had forgotten to call me right away when the call had come in. I still didn't think that that was crucial to what had happened, as I could just as easily have been delayed by a car accident or mechanical troubles.

"How is she?" I asked.

"Hollace," Paul said. "She's dead."

A short time later, I sat at the computer in my office and thought about Hollace and the broken hip that lead to her death. Then I thought of Ada's fall on the bathmat several months earlier and the events that both led up to and followed from it. When the paramedics had responded to the call, they'd asked for Ada's medical records. When one of the caregivers went to get her chart, they had given the paramedics the chart for a different Ada. This error was caught early by one of the hospital staff, before any harm could have been done by having the medical history, medication list, and allergies for the wrong person. When the caregiver had been asked about the mistake, he admitted he didn't know half the residents at Gleeful Meadows by name.

In every industry, whether you deal in goods or services, there are those in the company who work directly with the customers and clients, and then there are those who push paper. The paper pushers are necessary to the successful functioning of the business, yet, at the same time, they are once, twice, three times removed from the void in society filled by their products and services.

There was a disturbing trend that I had begun to notice at Gleeful Meadows. I suspect that it didn't exist solely at our community, but rather was characteristic of the senior care industry at large. To the majority of employees at the top of the food chain—managers, directors, chief operations personnel—the seniors whom we looked after were a means to an end: that end being profit. I don't fault them this. Without profit, there would be no jobs. Without profit, there would be no society.

What disturbed me was the growing number of staff on the ground level who had direct and meaningful contact with the senior residents of our community, but who saw them as little more than a way to make a paycheck. There were staff who didn't know residents' names, ones who would leave during shift to go take care of their own business, or quit on the spot because they didn't feel like adhering to the dress code. Most of the staff were wonderful, but that still did not negate the fact that I saw more and more in the halls at work, in all levels and departments, who couldn't care less whether they were in business to improve the lives of seniors or to sell bumper stickers by the side of the highway.

When I came out of my office, I ran into David N, one of our care staff. He had recently come back to work after a two-day suspension. An inspection during a night shift revealed that he had been having his wife come to Gleeful Meadows after she got off work to complete the laundry, cleaning, and cooking that he was responsible for, while he would lay around with his feet up, watching sports highlights.

"Hey, David," I said.

"You hear that Tonya got fired?" he said. "Because she wouldn't tuck in her shirt."

"Actually, she quit. Paul said she had to tuck in her shirt if she wanted to work. She just walked off."

"That isn't the way I heard it."

"I was there," I said. "But, anyway, did you hear that Grace died?"

"Is she the cook who got her leg run over?"

"No, our resident."

He stared at me blankly.

"She was council president. Always carrying around her oxygen tank, but never wearing her mask."

"All these old people look the same. Wrinkles, gray hair, and bad teeth."

I couldn't sleep that night. I sat at my computer desk and thought about what David had said. I was angry and hurt and offended, but I realized that he was not the one to be upset with. He couldn't help how he felt. The blame lay with those who would hire someone to care for old people who didn't really care for old people.

I typed the following email, that, by the next morning, had made its way into the inboxes of everyone from the janitor to the CEO of Gleeful Meadows.

Dear Colleagues:

How many of you have met James F? How about Jiro N? What about Willis P, or Clifford B? I'm not talking about checking their vitals or walking past them on your way to somewhere else. How many of you have actually met these people? Had a conversation with them? Gotten to know them? Made them feel welcome and part of the community?

Recently, one of our residents, Grace S, passed away. What surprised me was that some of our staff not only didn't know that she had died, but they didn't even know who she was to begin with.

It's easy for us to say that Grace refused to attend activities, or socialize, so what more could we do? That's the easy answer, but the wrong one.

We need to be engaging our residents on a regular basis, and not just the ones who show up to activities. All of us need to be going out of our way to make these people feel like they belong. That they are part of *OUR* community and that *WE* are a part of theirs. The fact that some of our residents sit in their rooms most of the time, or that they have diminished cognitive abilities, should not be an excuse for our lack of engagement in their lives. On the contrary, it should serve as a greater motivator to seek them out, not as an employee completing a job requirement, but as one member of a community reaching out to another.

At Gleeful Meadows, we use lots of euphemisms. We don't have a "receptionist," but instead a "concierge," and we don't work at a "facility," but a "community."

As you finish reading this email, ask yourself if we call ourselves a community because it sounds better on the brochure or because that's what we really are.

Kevin

I felt sick to my stomach as I drove into the parking lot at Gleeful Meadows the following day. I hadn't slept for most of the night, worrying about the effect, if any, that would come from the email I had sent. During the little sleep that did come to me, I was cast in a dream that my subconscious had clearly plagiarized from the movie "Jerry Maguire." I was Tom Cruise coming into work the morning after everyone had read his mission statement. Of course, the setting was Gleeful Meadows, and the coworkers were mine and not his, but I was still Tom Cruise and entered the workplace with the same trepidation he had clearly felt.

In a homoerotic twist, Eric gave me a back massage and used a printout of my email to wipe the extra lotion from his hands. Then I was called into Paul's office, where I had ninja stars thrown at me through an open window, though I couldn't see by whom. Apparently, this was the preamble to my firing. Paul told me to leave and that, if I took the ninja stars with me, I wouldn't receive my final paycheck. I pulled the bloody stars from my limbs and torso and handed them back to Paul without being able to look him in the eye. There was a purple Cadillac outside, which I assumed was already mine and not given to me as an exit-door prize. As I drove away with the ragtop down, a disembodied voice told me that I wouldn't be allowed to use my computer again, since I had made everyone so sad by what I had written.

What actually happened that morning was that I came to work early so that I could get into my office without having to talk with anyone. My email inbox was empty except for the copy of the email

I had sent that had been forwarded to me, as well, as soon as I clicked "EVERYONE."

The intercom on my desk phone beeped, and Paul's voice filled the air, "Are you there?" he asked.

"Can I say no?"

"Let's you and I have a chat."

Ten minutes later, I was in Paul's office, sitting across from him as he sipped his coffee and stared at his computer monitor. "It's harsh. Very harsh." He turned to me. "But underscores exactly how we've gone off track."

"Pardon?" I said.

"What do you think we should change?"

"I'm not fired?"

"Why would I fire you?"

"Is that a rhetorical question?"

"You're acting very strange," he said.

"Sorry, I just didn't sleep well."

"You've highlighted a very real problem with this email of yours. We work in a business where our business is people, and, to a large degree, we've lost sight of that. We all have. So, what do you propose we do to get us going back in the right direction?"

"Get the staff more involved with the residents. Did you know that most staff can only name about ten residents' names by heart? That's offensive."

"I'm guilty of that too," Paul said.

"Starting today, I think each staff member should have a five-minute conversation with a resident they've never met before. Then tomorrow do the same and continue this every day. Would that be so hard?"

Later that morning, Paul announced at a staff meeting that he wanted each of us to seek out a resident to have a chat with. Most people thought it was a great idea, probably since it meant they could put off their regular duties. After everyone dispersed to find a resident to chat up, I felt good about this new policy that I had helped initiate. This surely would make our community a more positive place to both work and live.

Then the crying began. Heidi, our office manager ran through the reception lounge toward her office and shut the door behind her. Wracking sobs could be heard from within. A few other staff members and I looked at each other in puzzlement. Shana knocked on her door. There was no answer. She slowly turned the knob and peeked inside. The crying didn't stop. She was either beckoned within, or invited herself, as she entered Heidi's office and closed the door behind her. They were in there for nearly a half hour before Shana again emerged. She didn't speak to us, but instead went quietly back to her own office.

I later learned that Heidi had been set off by her conversation with Chuck B, the first conversation she had had with a resident since coming to work at Gleeful Meadows. Chuck had told her of his life growing up on a cattle farm, on which he worked from as early an age as he could remember. He had gone to the local school, until his father withdrew him, so that he could work on the farm full-time. Shortly before leaving school, Chuck had taught his father how to read, and this remained the single greatest accomplishment of his life.

He told Heidi about his experiences during the depression and that, even though most people had to line up for hours in the hopes of acquiring even the most basic necessities for survival, he and his family were largely unaffected because they grew all their own food and fashioned their own supplies. He regretted turning people away who came to the farm either looking for work or food. "What else could you have done?" Heidi had commented. "Your family would have just starved along with everyone else."

Chuck spent his life on the farm, raising his crops and his cattle, and, eventually, his family. He likened himself to classic cowboys of cinema. His life, as he saw it, was perfect. Even when his wife passed away from breast cancer, he still saw his life as blessed. He had two daughters and a son, eight grandchildren, and thirty great grandchildren.

Then, earlier in the year, Chuck had had a stroke. He lost the use of most of his body and required assistance to do even the most basic tasks. He had gone from the tough patriarch of his family to a pitied old man, whom his family couldn't bear to look at. They moved him into Gleeful Meadows and have not yet visited. He believed it was because they couldn't bear to see the reality of the invincible father that still existed in their minds. He believed they wished he had just died and, similarly, his one wish, and the thing that he prayed to God for each night, was to die.

"He's a cowboy who shits in his own pants," Heidi said with a quivering voice. "It makes him sick just to see his own reflection. He asked me to help him die."

Heidi, too, grew up on a farm, and her own father had likened himself to silver screen cowboys. He was a year older than Chuck.

I was so pleased that I had initiated a plan that would lead to a better life for our residents, and likely a better work environment for our staff. If I could get them to care for those for whom they cared, then they might, in fact, enjoy coming in to work and see it as a rewarding experience for their soul and not just their pocketbook. The incident with Heidi and Chuck was just a hiccup. The morning visits by our staff with our residents would go on to inspire other senior care facilities.

That was the dream. In reality, that first day of individual visits with the residents was also the last time that that activity took place. The next day, too many of the staff members resumed their old game of senior avoidance and fell back into their own daydreams that removed them from the death, decay, and depression that they felt was all around them. They tiptoed behind the residents so as not to be noticed and engaged. They avoided eye contact with the blue hairs and, perhaps, held even a little animosity toward the geriatrics they saw for making them feel guilty and sullied in the first place. The handful of us who felt passion for our charges shrugged our shoulders and also fell back in line. Right behind our fearful leader, Paul, who was too concerned by the bottom-line to look up from his computer monitor and address the issue of apathy.

The next death came a week later. I was walking through the hallway in the Family Circle when Nicole came out of the room of Juliana M.

"Hi, Nicole," I said.

"Did you come to say goodbye?" she asked.

"To whom?"

"Juliana. She died about five minutes ago."

"I didn't know. Is she in there?" I gestured to her room.

"She's in her bed. Her daughter's in there with her. You can go in and say your goodbye."

"Oh, I don't know. I've never seen a dead person before."

"She just looks like she's sleeping. I know she meant a lot to you. She would have liked for you to say goodbye. I'll go in with you if you like."

I nodded.

Nicole took my hand and we entered Juliana's room. The overhead light was off and only a night lamp by her bedside illuminated the room. Laurena, Juliana's daughter, greeted me and we hugged.

"I'm so sorry about your mom," I said.

"There's nothing to be sorry about. This is a wonderful thing. She's at peace now, and I am so happy about that."

I turned to look at Juliana. Nicole put her arm around my shoulders as I moved toward the bed. She had been right. Juliana looked as though she were merely sleeping. Her eyes were closed, and her glasses lay on her night table. Her comforter was tucked underneath her arms, which were outstretched next to her body. I leaned forward and touched her cheek. It was cool to the touch.

"Goodbye, Juliana," I whispered.

Juliana had been a sweet lady, and Laurena was always so appreciative of the work that our staff did to take care of her mom. I thought of the fun I had had with Juliana, the time I had done a cartwheel in front of her and scared her, and the time I had bent over to help a resident out of a chair in the salon and Juliana, who was directly behind me in the hair dryer, poked me between the butt cheeks with her finger. When I turned to face her, she pretended to sleep.

I wasn't sad that she had died, as I hadn't known her well enough, though I wasn't glad like Laurena was either, also because I did not know her well enough. I don't know what I felt.

I have battled with my weight for most of my adult life. There have been periods where I have been in shape, though they have been short-lived, shattered by binge eating. I had lost thirty pounds for our wedding, and, in the year that followed, had put on forty. My unhealthy relationship with food, whereby I need to feel stuffed virtually every waking minute, was on a year-long honeymoon during the year that I worked at Gleeful Meadows. I had become good friends with the kitchen staff and, in so doing, had opened a reservoir of gastronomic splendor beyond anything I could have previously imagined. Most mornings, I would chat with Eric while helping myself to leftovers from the dining hall: hickory-smoked bacon strips, sausage patties, stacks of pancakes and waffles, scrambled eggs covered in cheddar cheese, or poached eggs with hollandaise sauce, with a liberal helping of hash browns. For lunch, the gluttony would be repeated with beef tips covered in blue cheese sauce, potatoes au gratin, blueberry pie, macaroni and cheese, spaghetti and meatballs, sweet and sour pork, mashed potatoes, and beef stroganoff. If, at the end of the day, there was any room left in my belly, it would be overfilled by the remnants of the dinner service: cheeseburgers, baby back ribs, burritos, nachos, clam chowder, country-fried steak, grilled catfish, meatloaf, and baked ham.

I had grown out of most of my clothes, and the button had popped off of most of my pants. I had begun pulling out my dress shirt just a little bit extra to hide the fact that my pants buttons were missing and that my belt was being stretched to its limit.

I didn't notice the weight gain as much as I would otherwise have, due to Angie's pregnancy weight gain. The only difference between mine and hers was that she would soon give birth to her extra weight, and I would be stuck with mine. In an effort to foster some weight loss motivation within myself, I created a poster in Photoshop that looked like a boxing advertisement. I had titled it "The Battle of the Bulge," and on one side of the photo was my face stuck onto the body of an overweight pugilist with the name "King-Sized Kevin" below it, and on the other side was Greg's face over the same overweight body with the name "Lard-Ass Greg." Greg and I had spoken about our mutual weight troubles, so I figured he would forgive whatever embarrassment the poster fostered and appreciate the motivation for weight loss that it started.

At the bottom of the poster, I described the specifics of the Battle: In order to raise money for the Alzheimer's Association, Greg and I would be hitting the gym. Residents, staff, and family members could donate to the cause and put in a guess at who would lose the most, how much we would each lose, and how much we would lose together. Those whose guesses were the closest would win a prize (no doubt something crappy from my activities budget).

I brought the idea to Paul, who immediately put down a hundred dollars that I would lose more weight than Greg. As soon as the posters were put up around Gleeful Meadows, the donations started rolling in. What had begun as a half-baked attempt to garner some external motivation to lose a few extra pounds had now become a serious challenge to my power of will and pride. Greg immediately changed his diet and stopped ducking into the Gleeful kitchen for snacks and meals. I knew I would have to force myself to do the same.

The biggest challenge I faced was a long-held inability to let any food in my immediate vicinity go to waste. I remembered the times as a child when I either didn't like what had been served to me or was too full to finish it and had been told that I had to finish every last bite before I could leave the table. *Kids are starving in China, you know.*

Now, years later, I sat on the curb in front of Gleeful Meadows at the end of the day, with a plastic bag containing running shoes, a tee shirt, and a pair of track pants. I sat on the cusp of a new, healthy lifestyle, yet couldn't work up the will to change into the clothes. Just maybe I could have started running right then in my slacks and dress shirt, but every excuse against action crept into my body and mind: I hadn't stretched, ate too recently, I'd look silly.

As I sat feeling sorry for myself and my inability to attain the body image I desired, Megan came along next to me and sat down. "What are you up to?" she asked.

"Aside from the obvious?"

"What are you *about* to be up to?"

"I was hoping to go for a run."

"Right, your battle of the bulge. I saw the posters. I put down five dollars that you'd smoke Greg."

"It's not going exactly well."

She fingered my plastic bag and saw my workout clothes within. "At least you brought your gear."

"That might be as far as I get today."

"What's the problem?"

"I just can't get myself moving. I know I could make a difference in my life right now, but either laziness or procrastination is standing in front of me."

"You need a drill sergeant."

"A drill sergeant? You mean a personal trainer?"

"No, I mean a drill sergeant. Not somebody to pat you on the back and put their hand on your shoulder. You need someone in your face, who won't put up with any bullshit."

"Angie doesn't have the time, but that sounds just like her."

"Well, how about I take on the role?" Megan asked.

"You don't need to go out of your way."

"Tomorrow, let's meet right here at the end of shift, and we'll go for a run together."

"You've got better things to do."

"Getting your ass in shape so I didn't put my money on a losing horse is as important as it gets."

"When you put it that way."

She stood and began to walk toward her car. As she walked, she turned to me and shook her finger. "Tomorrow. No excuses," she said. We smiled at each other as she got into her car and drove away.

That was the last time I ever saw Megan. She killed herself that night, and I found out about it when I walked into work the next morning. I often tried to imagine what could have happened between the time I last saw her and when she put that gun to her mouth. How bad could life have been for her? Was her depression chronic, or was it a feeling of despair that would have been washed away had she been alive to awaken the next morning?

In the weeks that followed Megan's death, I came to realize that we have far less influence over the lives of the people around us than we'd like to believe. That part of them that we see is often just a performance, or just an image that we ourselves cast upon them as an ideal. I wouldn't say that I exactly felt grief over her death. I'm not callous, I just didn't know her well enough to be anything more than shocked. What I did think about, however, were the obligations we have to one another and how fleeting they actually are. We have obligations to come to work, to make car payments, to help a friend lose weight, to pick up the tab the next time we meet our father for lunch—but what do these things really mean if they can't stop us from the most extreme way of breaking the obligation?

I found it hard to face the residents the day following her death. Firstly, I couldn't be cheery, as my job description entailed, but, more so, because I didn't know how to face their disappointment and sense of rejection. So many of them thought they had formed a special bond as well with Megan. Did those bonds mean nothing to Megan? Furthermore, how do you explain to people who had lived through wars and poverty that a young woman who had her entire life ahead of her had stolen that very future from herself?

CHAPTER THIRTEEN

Birth

It was finally time for our adventure out to the theater to see *Bye Bye Birdie*. Muana, one of our care staff, helped me load the residents onto the bus. She didn't look at me as she helped Cora up the steps. Mauna and I didn't much care for one another. She blamed me for receiving a one-day suspension from work. On one occasion, when I had filled in for Jennifer at the front desk, Muana had left her son there for me to watch over while she worked her shift. I told her that neither myself nor Gleeful Meadows were running a babysitting service. She said that her mother, who usually looked after her son while she was at work, was in the hospital. She asked if I could just watch him for an hour until her sister got off from work. I felt sorry for her for being in the position, like millions of others, of having to juggle work and the unpredictability of childcare. I promised that I would do my best to keep Paul from knowing that she had brought the boy to work. Luckily, Paul was busy elsewhere on the property, and the chances that he would be back in the reception area within the next hour were doubtful.

I provided the boy with some markers and paper and a mug of hot cocoa. Within a few minutes, he was out of control. He put his middle finger on the photocopier and set it for a thousand copies. Then, he went into Paul's office and began smacking his bongo drums. When I told him to stop, he came back into the reception area, hopped on the wheelchair of a resident who was currently in the beauty salon, and began racing around the tables and chairs.

I thought I could channel his energy, which seemed harmless, by asking him how long he thought it would take him to race around the building and then sending him off to do so. When he returned, I told him that I didn't think he could shave ten seconds off of his time. He was sure that he could and raced off to prove it. I had to leave the desk to assist the resident, who was now finished in the salon, back into her wheelchair. When I returned to the reception desk, I saw that the drawers had been rummaged and found Muana's little boy putting the money that was collected from selling stamps to residents in his pocket. I paged Muana to come retrieve her kid and told her what he had done. By now, Paul had returned and saw that the kid had used the felt markers on his bongo drums. He also saw that the drawers of his desk had been raided as well.

Angie and Ida, the daughter of Bernice, accompanied me to *Bye Bye Birdie*. They followed behind me in Ida's car and waited patiently while I parallel parked the bus right in front of the theater, much to the chagrin of every other driver on that street that night.

I had arranged for our residents to be brought in through a special entrance, meant for deliveries, so they could avoid having to circumnavigate the crowds. To this, Mildred protested, "I will not be led through some back entrance as though we're a gang of circus freaks." So, once we had gotten everyone else into their seats, I went around the front to escort Mildred in alongside the rest of the audience. It took us twenty-five minutes of waiting in line before we even made it to the ticket-taker. By then, Mildred's arthritis was aggravating her, and she was aggravating me by her incessant criticisms of people, places, and things.

When she and I finally got seated, Ida came alongside me and said that she and her mom needed to go. "She's really embarrassed about it. My mom pooped herself and wants to leave."

"I've got supplies in the bus. We can have her as right as rain in a couple of minutes."

"She said it's pretty bad."

"Tell her there's nothing to be embarrassed about. I've even got a change of clothes she can use. Please tell her not to leave."

Bernice walked over to us. "I'm going to go sit in the car. Ida, you stay and enjoy the show."

"Mom, I'm not letting you sit out in the car. If you're leaving, then I'll leave with you, but we can get you all fixed up."

"Down in front," Iris shouted at us.

"Oh, shut your face hole," Bernice said as she made her way to the aisle, where her walker was parked. Bernice continued to rant as she and Ida made their way out of the theater, accompanied by the voices of the performers on stage and a chorus of shushes from the audience members they passed.

I had not taken the length of the performance into account when I had selected it for one of our outings. I began to notice a great deal of fidgeting amongst my group. Then, finally, Norris Q stood, whirled around, and to the horror of the audience announced, "I've got to piss." The repeated restroom breaks and inability to remain in any one position for longer than a few minutes had Angie and me running through the aisles to usher our seniors back and forth between their seats and the restrooms.

On one of many trips back into the theater, a woman grabbed the sleeve of my shirt as I passed her in the aisle. "You've got a lot of nerve ruining our night out at the theater."

"It's a community playhouse, not Broadway. Get over yourself."

In the restroom, Norris couldn't see the wall in front of him, and, even though I had guided him into position, he reached out in front of himself and put his hand into the urinal.

Elsie refused to remove her long winter coat, even to go to the bathroom. Angie stood over her, after helping her onto the toilet, with a fistful of fabric so that it didn't end up in the toilet water or Elsie's urine stream.

"Oops, I didn't mean for the bowels to go," Elsie said.

Reflexively Angie pulled up a little harder on Elsie's coat, so it didn't get any of that on it as well.

When I got back to my seat, I performed a quick headcount and saw that one of my flock had strayed. I consulted my seat chart and discovered that the missing one was Iris. I turned and scanned the theater but didn't see her. I could feel the unfriendly stares of the other theater goers around me. I stood and ran up into the foyer. Iris was at the ticket window, "...well who am I supposed to be here with?" she asked the person behind the Plexiglas window.

"Iris," I said. "You're here with me."

"Oh, am I? Well, who's paying for this?"

"You are." I took her by the hand. "Come on, let's get back to our seats."

Overall, the trip was a success. Mildred, of course, complained that it was a sub-par theater troupe, Norris complained that he couldn't see anything, Hazel complained that she couldn't hear anything, and Iris was mad that she hadn't been invited to attend. Everyone else, however, was thrilled by the outing, which, for the evening, helped them feel as though they weren't so dependent on other people. I was still angry at Paul for not allowing me to take a caregiver with us to help out, but that feeling went away when, on the ride back to the community, Dorothea said, "It was so nice to have just you and your wife go out to the theater with us. It makes me feel like such an invalid when we have to have caregivers hovering around us all the time. With the two of you, it was like a night out with friends."

It was finally Friday, and I couldn't have been more relieved. It had been a long week. I looked at the activity calendar for the upcoming week and realized that, on several days, I had arranged too many activities too close together. I was no doubt destined to receive complaints from residents who had to miss the start of an activity because they couldn't hobble fast enough from one to the next.

I yawned and stretched with fatigue. I hadn't awoken the previous Monday morning with the usual sense of anticipation to arrive at work that I had felt for the past year. I hadn't gotten home the previous night until after two in the morning and had sat up most of the night with a head like hot soup. I was also a volunteer for the Seattle Police Department, where I helped victims of domestic violence. I had never previously had a problem leaving behind my experiences during my volunteer shifts when those shifts ended.

The previous night had been different. It was the first time I had responded to an incident where the victim was a senior. The woman whom the police had called us out to help was in her eighties and lived alone in the house she had grown up in. A year earlier, she had met a homeless man, who had come to her church for worship. She had felt a kinship with the man, as she had recently lost her only son to cancer. On several occasions, she took the man out for lunch after service. Then, one night, he showed up at her house and asked if he could stay with her for a couple of nights. The man had taken her generosity as a foregone conclusion, as he had already changed his address to hers with the DMV, SSA, and IRS. She found this out the next day, when mail began arriving for him. She told herself there was no harm in this, as long as it helped him get back on his feet.

Unfortunately, getting back on his feet meant sweeping hers out from under her. He began cashing her social security and pension checks and, eventually, stopped her from leaving the home. She was a prisoner in her own house and spent most of her time in her bedroom, as she couldn't bear to face the man whom she had initially felt kinship toward. Of course, she blamed herself for what she was going through. The police were called to the house when neighbors heard yelling. When they entered the home and found the woman, she could do nothing but cry.

It's wonderful that so many seniors are well enough and independent enough to live on their own, but the dangers that are out there hiding in the dark are numerous and unimaginable.

We were scheduled to play cards on the morning of Friday, April 6, though, instead, I took a group of residents to a doll museum. The doll museum had been scheduled for two days earlier, but I had made a last-minute change of plans on that day and taken them to visit one of our residents in the hospital. It was her birthday, and I didn't want her to spend it alone. It had begun as a way to avoid having to go to the doll museum, though that visit to the hospital ended up being one of the fondest and most rewarding memories I have of my time working at Gleeful Meadows.

I had brought a bus full of residents into the hospital room of Audrey D while she lay asleep. We stood around the bed, not wanting to wake her, yet not wanting to leave without wishing her a happy birthday. Cora clutched the ribbons of a dozen helium balloons, and Elsie, in her wheelchair, held a boxed birthday cake.

"Is she dead?" Iris asked.

"I think she's in a coma," Judy R said.

"She's not in a coma, she's just sleeping," I said. "We'll just wait until she wakes up."

"What happens if she doesn't wake up for the next few hours?"

"If she's not up in the next few minutes, I'm going to bump the bed," Iris said.

"She's a hardy sleeper."

"I don't think she's got her hearing aids in."

"Why's she in the hospital?"

"She's the one who likes her whiskey. I think she fell out of her wheelchair."

Suddenly, Audrey opened her eyes and looked up. She seemed to look around at each one of us, then closed her eyes and fell back to sleep.

"Well, that was anticlimactic," Cora said.

"Can we go now?" Iris asked.

"No," I said.

Bernice began knocking her knee against the side of the bed. "Wake up," she said. "It's time to eat cake."

Audrey opened her eyes again. "Oh, my goodness, what are you all doing here?" she asked.

"Happy birthday," we all shouted at her.

"Oh, my goodness." She shifted and reached over for the bed control. She used it to tilt herself upward so that she could see us all. "I can't believe you're all here. This is wonderful."

Elsie held up the cake. "This is for you to share with us, of course."

"You know, I woke up this morning and thought to myself, 'Well, Audrey, I guess you're going to have to spend your birthday all alone.' I'm so glad I was wrong. This is one of the best surprises I've ever had."

She reached out her arm, and I helped her swing herself to the side so that her legs could dangle over the edge of the bed. I pulled her wheelchair away from the side of the bed to give her some more room.

"When can you come back home?" Cora asked her.

"I'm not sure yet. They still don't know why I passed out yet."

"I pass out all the time," Iris said.

As they talked, I looked at my watch, knowing that I still needed to keep the activities for the rest of the day on schedule. Then, something on the floor caught my eye. It was a puddle of blood. I looked at Audrey's leg and saw a small tear in her calf that was squirting droplets of red. "Audrey, what happened to your leg?"

"You hit it with the wheelchair when you moved it."

"I'll get help," I said as I ran to the door.

"It's fine," she said. "It'll stop eventually. Come sit down and tell me what's been going on with all of you."

I ran into the hallway. "I need some help over here." I expected there to be a rush of medical personnel, but no one appeared. I ran to the end of the hallway and found the nurse's station. "I need some help in Audrey D's room. She's bleeding all over the place."

When the nurse and I entered the room, Audrey and the rest of the ladies were picking at the cake with plastic forks. No one seemed to notice or care that there was now a substantial amount of blood on the floor, and Audrey's leg and sock were now dyed red. The nurse knelt down next to her and began treating the wound. "Who did this?" she asked. What kind of a question was that? I wondered to myself. A normal person would have asked what had happened. Who walks into a room and asks, "Who did this?"

Cora pointed at me. "He did."

"It was an accident," I said. "And I don't even think the wheelchair bumped her. I didn't notice anything."

"It's okay," Audrey said. "I don't mind."

Everyone in the room was staring at me like I had farted...or like I had caused an elderly woman to bleed profusely onto the floor. Audrey's legs were swollen, with thinning skin that was already scarred from multiple abrasions. Really, it was an accident that she managed to do to herself frequently. This didn't negate the fact that I felt horrible. Audrey was in terrific spirits, and we continued to talk and laugh for the remainder of the visit.

Back at Gleeful Meadows, I sat alone on a park bench in the far end of the courtyard. I thought about the previous week, when Angie had thought her contractions had started. Instead, they turned out to be false. If they had been the real thing, I would have missed out on the experience with the ladies at Audrey's hospital bedside, which still, to this day, brings a smile to my face when I recall the smile it had brought to hers.

Arnold D came along next to me and lowered himself onto the bench. He was tall and lean, and, although he used a walker to get around, he had a tremendous air of dignity and grace. Arnold, a graduate of West Point, had retired as a colonel after a distinguished career in the military. Yet, with all his accomplishments, he was one of the most humble people I have had the pleasure of meeting.

"I'm still waiting for that game of handball," he said.

"Would I get to use a walker too?"

"Are you kidding? You don't have the kind of training these things require."

I felt sorry for Arnold, though I would never have insulted him by showing it. He didn't belong here. At least his mind didn't. He was cursed with chronic diarrhea, a family that lived far away, and a wife, who had been a homemaker, who died before she could impart upon Arnold how to use a microwave or a stove.

Arnold could survive off the land, fly fighter aircraft, and, in his earlier days, dance the waltz like his feet had been the property of God himself. Yet he never learned to look after himself in the nuances required to make it from one day to the next, and, for that, he was doomed to live out the rest of his days in the purgatory of assisted living, and in the care of folks like myself.

Arnold and I sat and watched as the sun dropped slowly behind a row of townhomes, sending out purple whorls into the sky above us. There was no hint that anything other than tranquility stretched out forever around us. But the truth was that the man who sat next to me was in pain. He was sad and angry and hated himself for feeling sorry for himself. Just a few feet away, Adeline, who looked out her window at us, felt alone and Elsie lay in bed wondering how much longer she could afford to remain at Gleeful Meadows before all her savings were gone.

Is that a dilemma that anyone should ever have to face? Hoping that they run out of life before their bank account does?

Somewhere within the walls of the Family Circle, Irene G took a spare donut off the snack table and tucked it into her jacket pocket to save for the husband she'd never see again; Stacie R, one of the care staff, hid her sick daughter in one of the empty rooms, neither able to leave her alone at home nor lose a day's pay to stay home to care for her; Paul sat at his desk wondering what type of care he could afford for his own father; two paramedics sat in their ambulance eating their dinner in the parking lot of Jack in the Box, each wondering what their families were doing at that moment, not knowing that, in a short while, their meal would be interrupted by a callout to Gleeful Meadows.

I hadn't yet decided what to make for Cooking with Kevin, but knew I had time to shop for the ingredients, as long as I could pick a dish relatively quickly. I took a book from my backpack called *Jewish Cooking*. The book, strangely enough, had been given to my non-Jewish wife by my one non-Jewish aunt. There wasn't any particular holiday I needed to cook for, but I thought it would be fun to try another Semitic dish.

The book was old and covered with stains—splashes of sauce and coffee rings. Opening the book let loose smells from different recipes that had been absorbed into the paper from years of use in the kitchen. I blew against one page, and a sprinkling of spice became airborne, dancing through the air and coming back around so Arnold and I could take in the fragrance. This was how I picked my recipe that day, because I could smell how each of the recipes was meant to be. On one page, I smelled cinnamon cake before I even read the name of the recipe. I turned another page with my eyes closed, and the essence of a rich beef stew entered my nostrils. Then cookies, chicken soup, crepes, and rugelach.

Following the activity, I took a piece of cake into the Family Circle for Wesley Marie. I found her in one of the lounge areas. She walked slowly toward the exterior door's keypad and pressed numbers at random. After this, she turned and walked the perimeter of the room before she returned to her place in a large armchair and sat. A few moments later, she got to her feet and again approached the keypad. She pressed numbers seemingly at random. Nothing happened. She walked the room and then retook her place on the seat. I watched her repeat this ritual for the next several minutes. She gave no evidence that she was aware of my presence.

I took the seat next to her as soon as she had lowered herself into the chair. I hated the chairs in the Family Circle. They were covered with a thick laminate to protect against the spillage of bodily fluids. Wesley Marie did not turn to look at me. I said hi to her, but there was no response. I put the piece of cake on a napkin upon the end table between us. Wesley Marie got up and returned to the keypad. After entering in a series of numbers, she completed her circuit of the room and then sat next to me. For the past several weeks, I had thought that Wesley Marie had lost the ability to speak or recognize those around her. Whenever I would ask if she remembered who I was, she would stare at me with a vacant expression. Her family, too, was met with similar results. Then, one of the care staff discovered something that gave us all hope that the woman we knew as Wesley Marie was still in there somewhere. When asked who a third person was, she answered immediately.

I pointed to my reflection in a mirror. "Who's that?" I asked.

"Kevin," she said.

"Who am I?" I asked. No answer. "Who are you?" I asked. No answer. I pointed to her reflection in the same mirror. "Who's that?" I asked.

"Wesley Marie," she said.

I picked up the cake and placed it on her lap. She looked down at it before getting to her feet. The cake fell to the floor. She did not seem to notice as she trod over it on her way to the keypad.

240

In the activity room, I set the drinks up on a large table next to an assortment of snacks that had been brought down by the kitchen staff. I ate a few pieces of cheese and washed them down with a glass of root beer. Before I knew it, the room was full of people, and Happy Hour was in full swing. Nicole was going from table to table, pulling residents to their feet to dance with her. I snacked a little bit more on finger foods as I served drinks. In the distance, there was a ringing. It continued for some time. I wondered where Jennifer was. Irritated, I walked into my office and to my desk and picked up the phone. "Good afternoon, Gleeful Meadows, Kevin speaking."

"Where the hell is Jennifer? I've been calling for the past ten minutes straight."

"Angie?" I said.

"My water broke."

"Really? Wow. How are you feeling?"

"I feel fine, but I'm leaking all over the place. I've already used up a box of pads."

"Do you want me to pick up some more after work?"

"What do you mean, after work?"

"What do you mean, what do I mean?"

"You've got to come home now."

"Now? I'm in the middle of Happy Hour here."

"What part of this whole baby thing don't you understand? My water has broken. This baby is coming."

"Holy crap," I said. For the record, I was really that naïve and didn't know that broken water meant "get your ass to the hospital." Luckily, Angie has common sense and paid attention during our prenatal classes.

I hung up the phone and ran back into the room full of seniors, my closest friends. I paused the music on the CD player. "Everybody," I called out. "Everybody. Angie just called. The baby's coming now."

There were cheers and applause, smiles and warmth. For many of the residents, those whose children and grandchildren and great grandchildren lived far away or never visited, Angie and I were surrogate family. This feeling was made even more palpable by the impending arrival of a child whom they had seen grow by way of Angie's belly during her visits over the past several months. It was truly their great grandchild who was on his way, if not by blood, then by emotion.

I grabbed some of my things that were close at hand and waved as I ran for the door. "Bye, everyone. Bye. I'll see you soon. Wish us luck. Don't cause too much trouble. Bye. Bye."

And that was it. I was gone. My last day of work with the seniors at Gleeful Meadows had come.

I have visited many times since then with Samuel, our son, and the residents, who are like family to us, relish in watching him grow. Though, for me, the visits are never as special as our time together when I worked there. I was replaced as activities director, and, in many ways, it felt like a new best friend had been hired for them. Really, that's what my job had been, to be their best friend…during business hours. Though, for me, it had happened for real, and I couldn't break the feeling.

When I arrived back at our apartment, Angie had already packed an overnight bag and was waiting for me in front of the TV.

"Are you okay?" I asked.

"Of course, I'm okay. Why wouldn't I be?" She stood to greet me, a towel wrapped around her midsection. We hugged and kissed.

"Were you at home when it happened?"

"No, I was out grocery shopping."

"Gross. Clean up on aisle seven."

"It wasn't like that. It's more like a constant trickle."

We hugged again.

"We're going to have a baby," I said.

At this point in the book, I would like to take this opportunity to give my condolences to all the women who had difficult pregnancies.

Don't hate us, but Angie had the easiest pregnancy we could have hoped for. No barfing from morning sickness, and a labor and delivery that could have been the description in a textbook.

As we sat waiting to be admitted, we were informed that all the triage rooms were full. This meant that we didn't have the hassle of later changing rooms, and we were immediately taken to our birthing suite.

The hours passed with nothing much of note taking place. Nurses came and went, and Angie had to watch as I ate meal after meal while reclined on a chaise in the corner of the room. A woman in the room next to us screamed as though she were being interrogated by the Gestapo. I took Angie for a walk through the hospital's corridors to take her mind off the labor pains and the screaming from the next room. I drew her a bath and ran a hot cloth over her neck. I ate another sandwich from the cafeteria and fought off sleep for as long as I could. When sleep did finally take me, my head fell back against the radiator on the wall next to me. I was the only one in the room who didn't hear the sound.

I awoke from a nap to different people in the room. I had slept through shift change. Angie now had a breathing mask on. I tried to rub the sleep from my head as I sat up.

She and the nurse turned to look at me. "You missed it," Angie said.

I stood and rushed to her. "Why didn't you wake me?"

"I wanted to let you sleep."

"Are you kidding me?" I knew I was a deep sleeper, but honestly, how pathetic to lie asleep in the corner of the room while your wife was giving birth. "Where is he?"

"Where's who?" she asked.

Was I still asleep? "Our son."

She looked at me confused. "Still in my belly. Where else would he be?"

"So, what did I miss then?"

"My blood pressure dropped, so they had to give me an oxygen mask."

243

"Holy crap, crazy lady. I thought you meant you gave birth."

"And let you sleep through it, are you kidding me?" She and the nurse shook their heads at each other. *Men.*

It was about at that point that the screaming began. Not Angie's, but the woman in the room next to us once again. Angie put her pillow over her head. "I can't take it anymore. Would somebody please do something about that woman? She's freaking me out. Is that what I'm going to have to go through? Can't they give her something? Put her out of her misery? Put me out of my misery?"

The hours crawled by. It was again shift change, and a new nurse came into the room. There was a guy with her. "Is it alright with you if I have a student shadow me during your care?"

Before I could say a thing, Angie said it was alright.

"Hi, I'm Raheem," the trainee said as he stuck out his hand.

I shook it.

"You're training to be a nurse?" Angie asked.

"I'm training to become a nurse's aide," he said. "One day I'll go to school to become a nurse."

There was a whole lot more waiting before anything further happened. The nurse instructed me on how to count along while Angie pushed. The doctor came in and saw that very little was happening, so he left to see other patients.

I began to make small talk with Raheem to pass the time. "Are you enjoying your training?" I asked.

"Very much. I've always wanted to work in labor and delivery."

"It must be very rewarding being there for the birth of people's babies."

"Actually, this will be the first birth I'll be present for. I'm very excited."

"You don't currently work in a hospital?"

He shook his head. "Currently I work in assisted living."

I couldn't believe it. "Hey, great! I work in assisted living too," I said. "Where do you work?"

"It's called Gleeful Meadows," Raheem said.

The smile dropped from my face. "That's where I work."

"That's wonderful. What a wonderful coincidence."

Wonderful was not the word I would have used to describe it. "How come I've never seen you?" I asked.

"I work the night shift. I'm a caregiver there."

A short time later, when Raheem and our nurse were on the other side of the room, I leaned in close to Angie. "I don't know how cool I am anymore with this guy, Raheem, checking out your vagina."

"He's not checking out my vagina. You said you were okay with him observing."

"That was before I knew he was a coworker."

"Give me a break. You don't even work there anymore."

"It's only been a few hours since I've left. I didn't even clock out."

"It's fine."

"Fine? What if he says something to someone?"

"You're being ridiculous."

"Does this mean you'd be fine with all the staff there checking out your goodies? Should I give Paul and Greg a call?"

"You're being silly. Stop it."

I turned to Raheem who had gone from being a sweet guy to a lecherous pervert.

Angie finally asked for an epidural, and all the pain she was experiencing (except for me) went away as though it had never even been there at all. She was also still barely dilated, so they gave her an injection of oxytocin to speed things along. And speed things along it surely did. She went from two centimeters dilation to ten centimeters in a matter of minutes.

It was now time for our baby to arrive. I instructed the nurse that I didn't want to see any blood and wished to pass the torch of cutting the cord on to anyone else.

As Angie began to bear down, and I began to count, a faint ringing sounded out. I looked around but didn't see where the ringing was coming from. "Should something be ringing?" I asked the nurse.

She shook her head.

Angie turned to me, "That sounds like a phone."

I looked down next to me and saw a small cupboard recessed into the wall alongside the bed. I opened it and found the ringing phone. "Hello?" I said as I answered it.

"Hi, Kevin. Just checking in to see how things are going." It was my stepdad.

"Now's not really a good time," I said. "Angie's giving birth right now. That's why our cell phones were turned off. Gotta go. Bye."

"Well then what are you doing on the phone with me?" he said before he hung up.

Angie continued to push as I continued to count. The doctor came into the room to check on Angie's progress, looked between her legs and said, "Oh my, we're having a baby in here."

I looked at the joy on Raheem's face, the sheer excitement at being present as our child was coming into the world. Although I was up next to Angie's head, holding her hand, and trying not to see anything nasty, I felt so much a part of the awe and wonder of childbirth as I vicariously fed off of the expressions of excitement and wonder of everyone else who were (no pun intended) in the trench.

We called our son Samuel, giving him the middle name Wesley to honor my good friend Wesley Marie.

We spent the night, our little family—Angie, Samuel, and I—in Angie's hospital room. As I slept, more fatigued from emotion than lack of sleep, Angie took pictures of Samuel and me. She took close ups of his tiny feet and hands, focusing in on the lines and creases. Angie always seemed to have such a remarkable store of energy, and having just given birth was no exception.

I awoke just after dawn. Angie lay asleep in her bed and Samuel in his. They both seemed so delicate and the moment so perfect, and it was as though, if I blinked or turned away, their fragility would forever rob me of them. The day would be a busy one, this I knew. Soon we would leave the hospital and return to our little apartment, which would now be even smaller as a home for three. There would be visits from family and friends, phone calls, and, of course, the ever-present knowledge that we were now responsible for a being wholly dependent upon us. I thought of work—my now former work—and the title the industry held: assisted living. In that moment, I realized that we all needed assistance in living. None of us could do it alone, in a vacuum apart from the influence and guidance of others.

I touched Samuel's head. I was in awe of what we had created. It seemed impossible to me that he could be so perfect. I thought, once again, about all that could go wrong with the delicacy of life, then I was reminded of the fact that the odds were always in the favor of health. The miracle of life is that perfection is the rule and not the exception.

I smiled. I had no idea what to do with this little person that would now rely upon Angie and me for everything. Soon we would be on our own.

In the weeks that would follow, I would become more comfortable and proficient in my role as a stay-at-home daddy. I would come to know the meaning of every sound that my little son made. I would be there for him at night, when he awakened in tears, and during the day, when all he wanted to do was have fun and play. I would take my son to Gleeful Meadows for visits and, finally, get that elusive hug from Bernice W, the cooing of a newborn infant making her weep in my arms. I would listen in the darkness at night for the sound of his snoring. I would play with his toes while he laughed as though it were the funniest thing in the world. But that was all for later. Right now, there was just the sunrise and the giddiness that comes with being on the cusp of a new experience, one we weren't sure we were ready for, but were too excited about to care.

I stepped out into the hallway and turned on my cell phone. I dialed Gleeful Meadows and waited. Shana answered.

"It's Kevin," I said.

"Congratulations, new daddy."

"Thank you."

"When can we see the little one?"

"Soon." I pulled Angie's hospital room door closed behind me so that she wouldn't awaken to the sound of my voice. "I just wanted to call to make sure someone was going to take care of the activities today."

"Kevin, listen to me very carefully. You don't work here anymore."

"I know, I just—"

"You don't work here anymore. It's not your problem. Let things happen without you. Go be with your family and let go of this place. They need you, and we don't."

After I ended the call, I stood motionless for quite some time, absorbing Shana's words. I had become obsessed with my work. It had become my life, and now I felt lost without it. But that would change. I had a new life and new horizons to look forward to, but I knew the adjustment would take time. My job meant so much more to me than I can articulate in words. I truly feel that it saved my life. Before I came to work at Gleeful Meadows, I truly felt that I was just killing time until my own retirement or death. My life had become a means of killing time. I didn't enjoy my day-to-day existence because I felt my life was void of purpose. That job gave me purpose. Although the focus was different, I often thought of my fortune at finding my place at Gleeful Meadows in the line of the song "Amazing Grace." *I once was lost but now am found.*

I quietly pulled open the hospital room door and looked in at my sleeping wife and son. *I once was lost but now am found.*

I entered the room and closed the door. I kissed Angie on the forehead and did the same for Samuel. His lids opened, and with unfocused eyes, he looked around the room. As I stood over him, I suddenly smelled an odor emanating from him. I leaned toward him and saw that he needed to be changed. I retrieved a fresh diaper from a nearby cupboard and tried to remember what I had learned about changing a diaper in the parenting class.

As I removed the diaper, I looked down at the smiling face of my son—his expressive eyebrows and the dimple in his cheek that he got from Angie. He was so fresh and new that his fingernails and toenails hadn't even completely grown out yet. At that moment, I felt the greatest sense of joy, a kind that I never would have thought possible. I thought about the revolutions of fate, the twisting of the universe, and the spiraling of our planet and all the forces that had put me here, now, into this place and position, with my very own set of poopy fingers.

The End